MW01625558

# A Journey Through the Maxwelton Watershed

*A Natural and Social History*

*Written by Ann Linnea*

*Published by the*

**Maxwelton Salmon Adventure**

Whidbey Island, Washington

2002

Produced through funding from the Public Involvement & Education Project, financed by proceeds from the Washington State Water Quality Account and administered by the Puget Sound Water Quality Action Team.

This book is part of a larger Maxwelton Salmon Adventure project called "Remember the Past, Envision the Future." Many thanks to the Puget Sound Water Quality Action Team for their moral and financial support for this history project, and to Laura Fox who had the original concept for it.

Thanks also to the Advisory Committee who helped steer the entire project and who reviewed the book manuscript through many drafts. Members of the board, staff and friends of the Maxwelton Salmon Adventure made valuable contributions through their energy, expertise and comments on the manuscript. Thanks to the South Whidbey Historical Society, to Island County Public Works staff, and to everyone who provided information or photos or helped in any way on this book.

Maxwelton Salmon Adventure is so grateful to Ann Linnea for her thoughtful, enthusiastic writing and to Vicki Grayson Liden for her creativity and persistence. We were blessed to have them involved!

Every attempt has been made to verify information presented in this book. Please report any errors or omissions to the Maxwelton Salmon Adventure at any of the contacts given below. A feedback form is included with this book—your comments are welcome!



**A Journey Through the Maxwelton Watershed: A Natural and Social History**
*Written by* Ann Linnea
*Edited by* Nancy Waddell
*Book design & layout by* Vicki Grayson Liden, Grayson Design
*Copy editing by* A.T. Birmingham-Young
*Cover, Anthes cabin, and glacier illustrations by* Susan Zwinger

*Published by*
The Maxwelton Salmon Adventure
P. O. Box 617 ~ Langley, WA 98260
(360) 579-1272 ~ info@salmonadventure.org ~ www.salmonadventure.org


First printing 2002
Produced in the Maxwelton Watershed of Whidbey Island, Island County, Washington
Printed in the United States of America

ISBN 0-615-12262-0

# Table of Contents



*And the journey begins...*

MAXWELTON WATERSHED
LEGEND
WATERSHED BOUNDARY
WETLANDS
STREAMS
WATER TYPES 1-4
WATER TYPES 5-9
AUGUST 2002
N
S
E
W
COLES
MAXWELTON
PIONEER PARK
MILLER LAKE
MAXWELTON CREEK
EWING
CAMPBELL
SR 525
CULTUS BAY
QUADE
QUADE CREEK
SILLS
FRENCH
BAILEY
GLENDALE
SWEDE HILL
Vancouver Island, B.C.
San Juan Islands
Bellingham
Whidbey Island
Victoria
Strait of Juan De Fuca
Everett
Olympic National Forest
Seattle
Hood Canal
Tacoma
Pacific Ocean
Olympia

# Acknowledgements

Many, many people contributed to this book. First, a special thank you to all of the people willing to be interviewed and share what they know about Maxwelton. Talking with you was a wonderful privilege.

Members of the watershed history project advisory committee gave generously of their time and talent to direct and edit the writing of this book: Barry Bjork, Carolyn Geise, Russell Link, Bruce Morrow, Todd Peterson, Virginia Price, Bud Silliman and John Williamson.

Several longtime Maxwelton residents read portions of the book and provided valuable insight and direction. Thank you to Gerry Brixner Miller, Myron Brixner, Evelyn Hagstrom Varon and Darrell Green.

Project director Nancy Waddell was amazing! Any time of the night or day she cheerfully provided invaluable direction, assistance and guidance. Maxwelton Salmon Adventure staff person Laura Fox was a helpful editor and resource person. A special thank you to the following people for editing help above and beyond the call of duty: Christina Baldwin, Russell Link and Todd Peterson.

The writing of any book is an enormous responsibility, for the printed word takes on an element of truth or fact that shapes the reader's worldview. This is particularly true for a history book. I worked as carefully as I was capable of to craft a book that accurately tells the history of a place that I cherish.

Many hands helped direct the vision of this book, but ultimately the emphasis I have chosen to place or not place on certain stories, facts and events is the product of my own worldview and perspective. I appreciate growing up in a rural farming area, so that I might better understand the joys and challenges of life in Maxwelton. So, I dedicate this book to my parents, Astrid and Frank Brown, who raised me up with old-fashioned values and a deep, abiding love of place.

***– Ann Linnea***

Although the Maxwelton watershed wasn't named until after 1905 when the Mackie brothers arrived, the area was geographically a watershed long before that. The Native American name for this area is unknown. We have used the name Maxwelton to denote the entire watershed regardless of time period to be clear to the modern reader. Names of modern roads are also used although they may not have been the original designations.

*Maxwellton braes are bonnie*
*Where early falls the dew*
*And it's there that Annie Laurie*
*Gi'd me her promise true.*
*Gi'd me her promise true*
*Which ne'er forgot will be*
*And for bonnie Annie Laurie*
*I'd lay me down and die.*

"Annie Laurie" by William Douglas/Lady John Scott

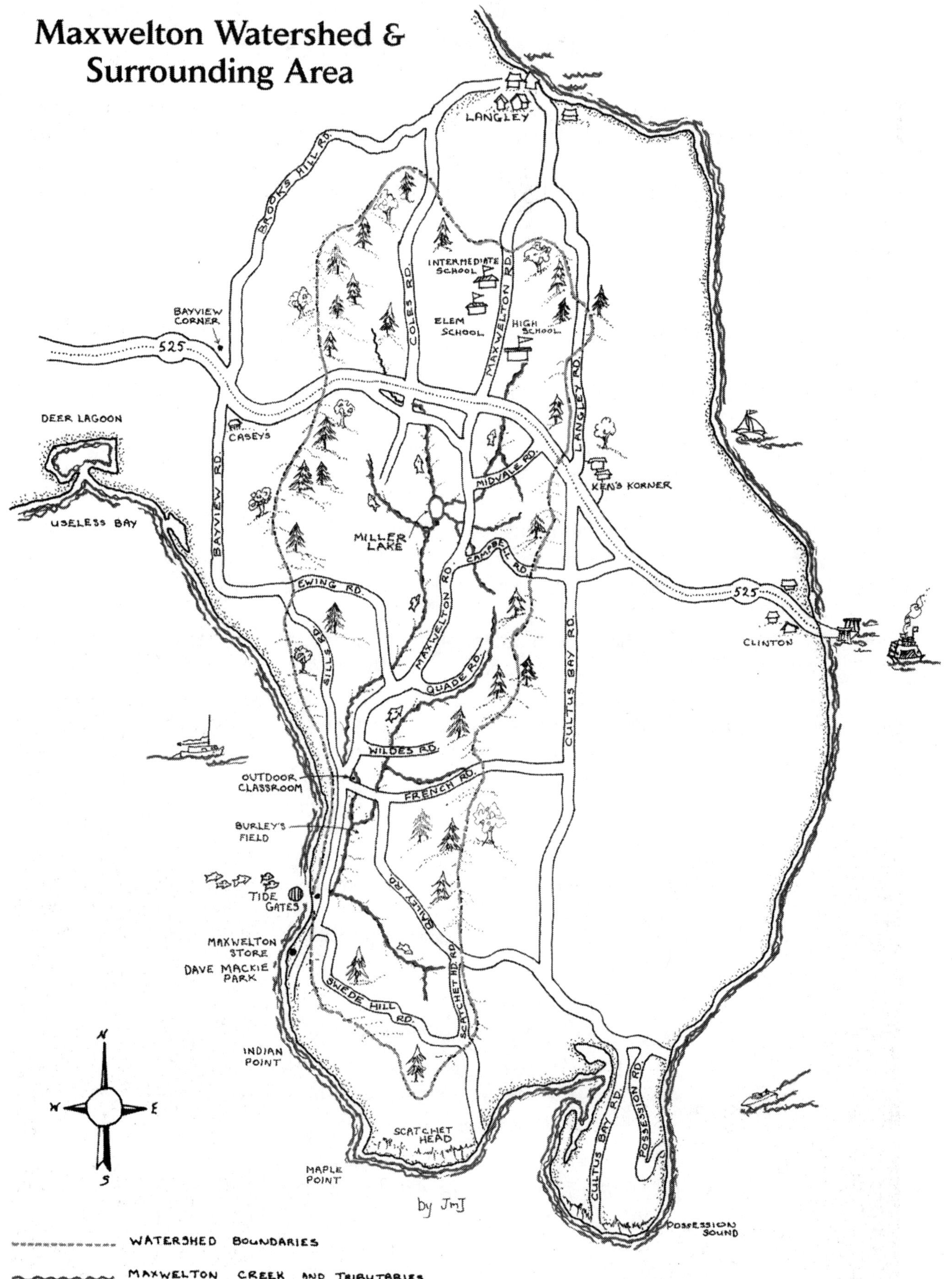
Maxwelton Watershed &
Surrounding Area
LANGLEY
BROOKS HILL RD.
COLES RD.
INTERMEDIATE SCHOOL
ELEM SCHOOL
HIGH SCHOOL
MAXWELTON RD.
BAYVIEW CORNER
525
LANGLEY RD.
DEER LAGOON
CASEYS
BAYVIEW RD.
MIDVALE RD.
KEN'S KORNER
USELESS BAY
MILLER LAKE
CAMPBELL RD.
EWING RD.
CLINTON
SILLS RD.
MAXWELTON RD.
QUADE RD.
CULTUS BAY RD.
WILDES RD.
OUTDOOR CLASSROOM
FRENCH RD.
BURLEY'S FIELD
TIDE GATES
BAILEY RD.
MAXWELTON STORE
DAVE MACKIE PARK
SWEDE HILL RD.
SCATCHET HD RD.
N
W
E
S
INDIAN POINT
SCATCHET HEAD
MAPLE POINT
CULTUS BAY RD.
POSSESSION RD.
by JmJ
POSSESSION SOUND
WATERSHED BOUNDARIES
MAXWELTON CREEK AND TRIBUTARIES

# Introduction

People in the Pacific Northwest are generally aware of Whidbey Island. As the largest island in the contiguous United States, Whidbey makes a 38-mile serpentine stretch from Deception Pass on the north to Cultus Bay on the south. At its southern terminus it is some thirty miles north of Seattle. Near that southern edge lies the island's largest watershed—an area relatively unknown by those not living on Whidbey.

Yet, the history of Whidbey Island's Maxwelton watershed and the issues facing it today stand as a template for most regions of the Pacific Northwest. Examining its environmental history and looking at some of the issues it faces, may offer some insights to people living in other watersheds of this region.

The historical and current existence of salmon in Maxwelton Creek has made this book possible. At the same time, salmon are one part of current land use controversies. There are fourth- and fifth-generation farmers still actively farming in Maxwelton. These are people who deeply love, understand and respect the land. They are primarily responsible for preserving the rural atmosphere of South Whidbey Island. Yet many of the regulations that challenge their ability to continue to farm their lands exist to protect the salmon quality of Maxwelton Creek.

This book honors these pioneering families and seeks solutions to maintain their way of life as well as preserve Maxwelton Creek as a salmon stream. This is a tall order, but the Maxwelton Salmon Adventure believes such a broad focus is in the best interests of the land, people and creatures of this beautiful Northwest valley.

In the short time frame of the writing of this book it was impossible to trace the lineage of all founding settlers of the valley. Those mentioned here have current living relatives or their histories were obtained through other written works about South Whidbey. All early settlers made important contributions. Apologies to those not covered here.

A Journey Through the Maxwelton Watershed

Chapter 1

# From Glacial Beginnings

It's April 2002. A cold, intermittent rain sweeps across the Maxwelton marsh on the south end of Whidbey Island near Useless Bay. The wind picks up off the frigid waters of this northern part of Puget Sound and one can almost imagine a receding glacier lying just beyond the next bay.

Along the northwest edge of this marsh there is a farm field that used to belong to Leon Burley. Leon tended this twenty-acre parcel for most of the twentieth century. His spirit of care and love for this place still resides here as surely as if he were driving his old jeep down from his house on the ridge to round up cows for their nightly feeding.

Burley's field lies between two ridges and is bounded by Maxwelton Creek and Quade Creek. It contains as fine an access to marsh wildlife as one can find on the island. Even on this cool April evening frogs, coyotes, beaver and a wide array of birds can be seen and heard.

The stealthy silhouette of an owl flying low on its first hunt of the night signals the beginning of dusk. The wings of small, green-winged teal ducks whistle toward a splash landing in the beaver ponds to the east, as waterfowl resettle on their nightly resting spots. Larger, slower-moving mallards settle in next. And nearly every night a loud, guttural squawk cuts the dusk as a great blue heron comes to roost in a stand of alders along Maxwelton Creek.

The history of this marsh is peopled by men and women who knew the watershed as thoroughly as the heron knows it. First there were the native tribes; then, for the last century-and-a-half, European-American settlers have roosted alongside the creek and its marshes.

The wind and rain on this evening make it difficult to hear the heron's squawk, but the weather helps hold the focus on the marsh itself. Dusk is many shades of gray. Rain is many degrees of wet. The marsh exhales a muddy breath as it seeps into shadow. Car lights making their way up French Road to the north seem like a surreal apparition rising out of the ancient scene of this marshland. The glaciers that formed it feel very close.

## The Last Great Glacier

Three waves of glaciers helped form Puget Sound. The last of these, the great Vashon Glacier, began about 20,000 years ago when ice from the coastal mountains of British Columbia began moving toward the area that later became the U.S. border. This dramatic ice and snow event helped shape the Maxwelton watershed.

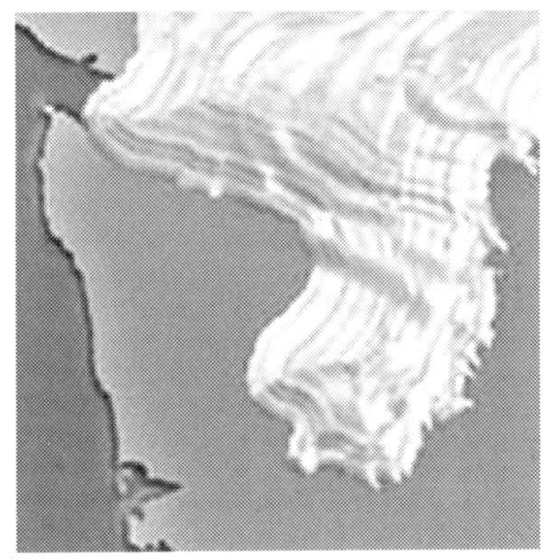

*The mile-thick ice of the Vashon Glacier reached as far as Olympia where it merged with smaller glaciers coming down the flanks of the Olympic and Cascade Mountains.*

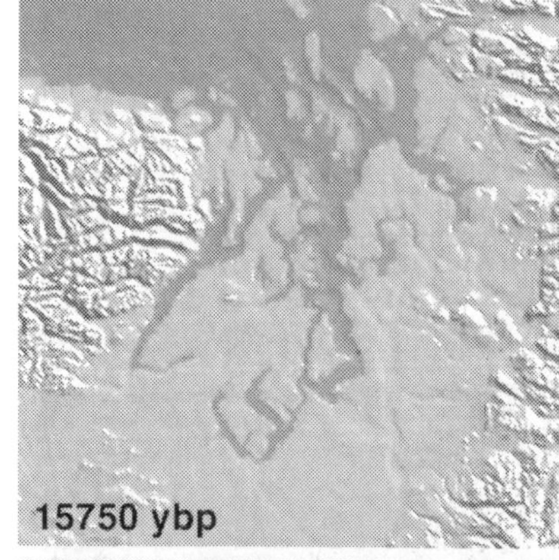


A watershed is an area of land that drains to a common point like a river, a stream, or to salt water. The drainage system of the Maxwelton watershed conveys rainfall to Puget Sound through the Maxwelton Creek. Swede Hill, Kyllonen Hill and the hill to the west of Miller Lake are the "hallways" that catch and direct rainfall and spring-flow down to the creek.

Watersheds generally change gradually, and in Whidbey Island's mild climate are not affected much by snow and ice. But this glacial ice was different.

The Puget Lobe of the Vashon Glacier, with ice believed to be one mile thick, reached its southernmost extent below Olympia about 17,000 years ago. The ice compressed—squeezed and submerged—the land beneath it. As the climate gradually warmed, the Vashon Glacier retreated northward—at the rate of about one mile every 25 years—faster than it had moved southward.

By 15,000 years ago the glacier had receded back to the Canadian border but much of present day Whidbey Island, including what would one day become Leon Burley's field, remained under water. It would take another four to five thousand years for the low spots on Whidbey to recover from the compression of the ice and for the level of a flooded Puget Sound to slowly lower.

### Life Returns

During those four to five thousand years, vegetation gradually returned to the high hills of what was becoming the

*Watch Whidbey Island emerge and change as the land springs back after Vashon Glacier recedes. (ybp=years before present)*

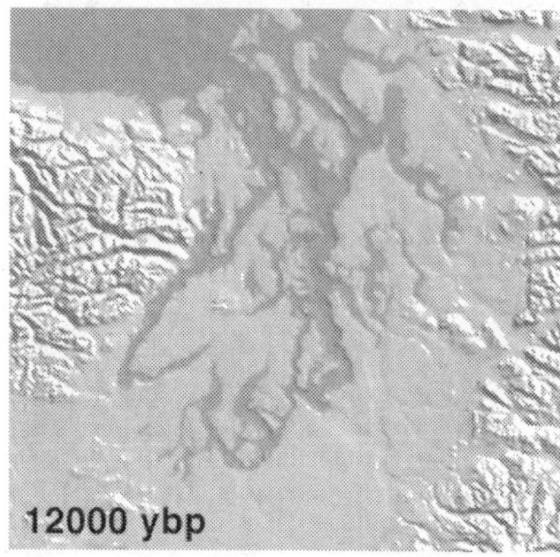


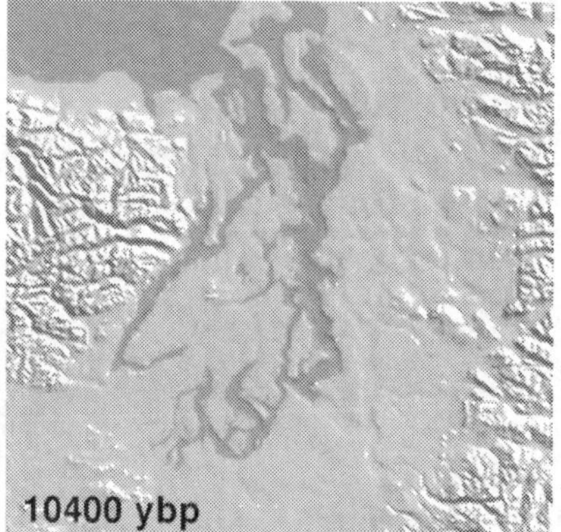


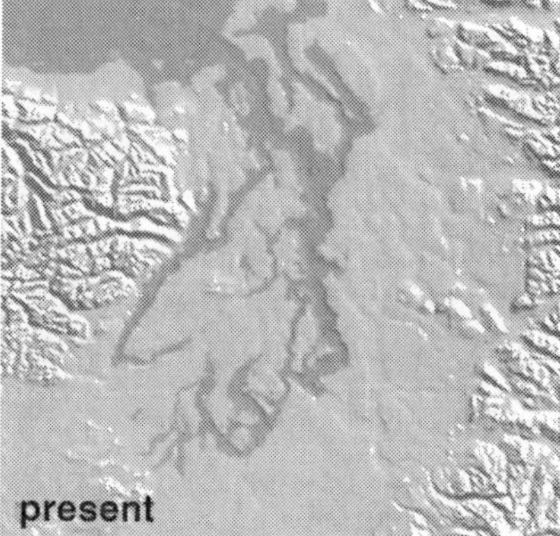

Maxwelton watershed. At first the valley was still an arm of Puget Sound extending well inland of Miller Lake. As the water retreated and the land "sprung back," the vegetation spread slowly down the slope of the hills into the waterlogged valley. Mosses were among the early plants readily adapted to living in these cool, moist, low-lying conditions.

Animals were also arriving in the fledgling watershed. The tiny, mouse-like shrew is one of the present-day animals that may have come here then. Biogeographers--those who study the geographical distribution of living things--believe their arrival was influenced by the last ice age.

In one theory, Whidbey Island may have been connected to the mainland coast at the end of the Vashon glaciation when sea levels were lower on parts of the coast. Shrews could have then reached the island over land and become isolated when sea levels rose. Shrews may have also reached the island on an ice bridge created by the receding glacier.

Another explanation is that shrews colonized Whidbey Island more recently, crossing Puget Sound by rafting on floating logs or debris. (Shrews have been known to cross water barriers of several kilometers in freshwater lakes.) The presence of shrews on Puget Sound islands remains one of the unexplained mysteries of island biogeography.

## Glacial Remnants

Numerous relics from the time of the glacier remain in this area. Along the Maxwelton shore and other areas of Whidbey it is easy to find dark gray rocks with beautiful white lines. These rocks were carried down from British Columbia by the Vashon Glacier as it scoured the landscape and formed a moving edge of ice, rock and gravel. As the glacier retreated and melted, it left these and other small rocks and it left some large boulders. These huge "glacial erratics" can be seen on many Whidbey Island beaches and fields. One of the largest lies between Indian Point and Maple Point, to the south of the Maxwelton beach.

More remnants of the glacial era in the watershed are the many deposits of peat—partially decayed plant matter in wet ground. There are extensive peat deposits around Miller Lake (a remnant of a much larger lake) and on the east side of the lower watershed. This peat was formed by the compression of plants by the glacier and decay of mosses and other primitive plants that grew after the glacier. The tannins (plant acids) found in peat give Maxwelton Creek its distinctive brown color.

*Examples of hardened peat from older glaciations can be found on the beaches at the south end of Whidbey Island. Harold Overton examines a sample on a geology hike at Maple Point.*

Beachcombers, particularly those on beaches from Possession Point to Scatchet Head to Double Bluff, are also intrigued by the remnants of woolly mammoths. Teeth, bones and even entire tusks have been found imbedded in local cliffs.

"Woolly mammoths roamed the Puget Sound area from 10,000 to a couple of million years ago," explains John Elverum, Clinton amateur paleontologist. "There were a number of glacial periods during that long time span. Each time, some mammoths were killed and others managed to retreat, survive and return. Fossils imbedded in local cliffs are likely from mammoths that lived in the area and were killed during earlier glacial ages."

Elverum says that evidence of mammoths from the most recent (Vashon) glaciation is hard to find because most of the bones haven't yet gone through fossilization—turning to stone. But he says that in all likelihood mammoths roamed the Maxwelton watershed for a time after the last ice age.

## Trees and Fish

The question of which re-established first on the barren post-glacier landscape—plants or animals—is a scientific puzzle that sheds light on what the early watershed looked like. Mammoths certainly were in the area very soon after the glacier retreated and to range here they required a food source.

Using pollen analysis—since, as Elverum explains, "There simply aren't many plant fossils in this area"—paleobotanists have determined that lodgepole pine appeared almost immediately after the glacier. This species matures early, seeds prolifically and thrives in a wide range of conditions.

*Lodgepole Pine*

As the glacier retreated further northward and the climate began to stabilize, other tree species appeared that could outlast the short-lived lodgepole. Scientists estimate that over a three- to four-thousand year period Douglas fir replaced lodgepole as the dominant species.

Salmon was another important early species to return to the barren landscape in the lee of the Vashon. "Pacific salmon are believed to have survived the most recent glaciation in two refuges, one each on the North American and Asian continents," writes Bruce Brown.

"With the glacier's retreat 10,000 years ago, the salmon fanned out and recolonized millions of miles of rivers draining into the North Pacific." Brown explains that the salmon brought nutrients from the sea to the land by dying after spawning. These nutrients were important in re-establishing vegetation in the watershed.

With the return of salmon and the establishment of a wet climate, western hemlock and red cedar began to advance from pockets where the glacier had not destroyed them. The shade-loving seedlings of hemlock and cedar began to take hold underneath a canopy of Douglas firs.

Sitka spruce grew up along the peat bogs of early Whidbey Island. Red alder, ash, and maple located along flood plains, shorelines and the banks of streams like Maxwelton Creek.

Over time, the returning plants and animals created an ecosystem that began to support insects, birds, reptiles, amphibians, mammals and eventually people. One can imagine this ecosystem all coming together on the marsh edge where Burley's land is located, where salt water continued to invade until the era of dikes.

### Humans Arrive

The oldest sites of human habitation excavated in this region are dated at 10,000 to 12,000 years ago and rest directly on glacial till—evidence that people arrived even before significant vegetation had returned. Similar-aged sites have been found at Cattle Point on San Juan Island and at Cornet Bay facing Deception Pass.

These early "glacier" people were gradually replaced by the Salish, who were here before white settlers came to the area. The Salish, who call themselves "people of the canoe," were dominant in the region by 1300 of the Common Era.

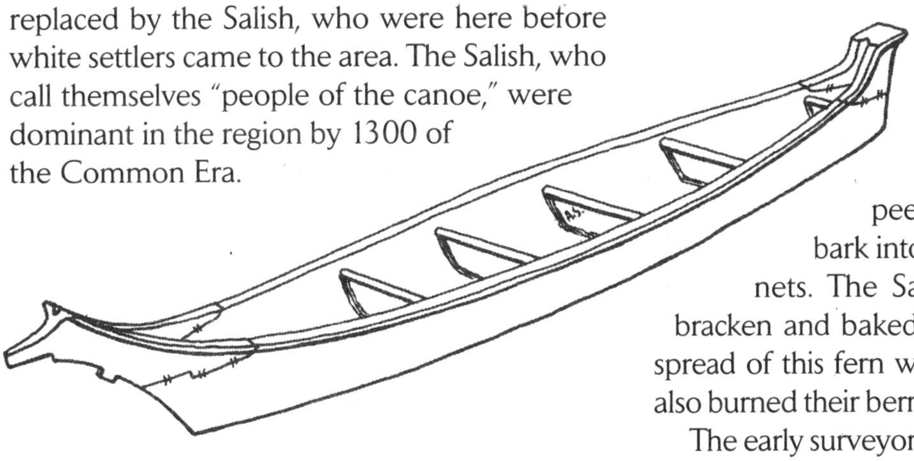

The Snohomish tribe of the Salish peoples occupied the southern end of Whidbey Island. These people developed permanent longhouse settlements at Bush Point, Sandy Point and Cultus Bay and did extensive berry collecting, hunting and fishing in areas like Maxwelton. They were called the Snohomish because the bulk of their salmon fishing was done at the mouth of the Snohomish River in what is now Everett.

North and central Whidbey were occupied by the Skagit tribe, who fished the Skagit River for salmon. However, all of these people also fished out in the Sound and even into the Straits of Juan de Fuca, as the weather permitted.

Although the earliest white settlers believed that the marsh, the forests and even the prairies of central Whidbey were virgin land, there is much evidence to suggest that the Salish had somewhat altered the landscape by using both cultivation and fire.

When white surveyors arrived on Whidbey in the 1850s, they discovered three plants in abundance—bracken fern, nettles and camas—and were aware that the natives were in the practice of burning the prairies. Closer examination of the native villages revealed tended nettle patches, which were burned at the end of the season.

Anthropologist Erna Gunther credits the Salish with using over fifty varieties of plants. They made medicines and dyes from the nettle plants and peeled, dried, and rolled the bark into string for fishing and duck nets. The Salish ground the roots of bracken and baked the flour into bread. The spread of this fern was aided by burning. They also burned their berry patches to increase yields.

The early surveyors of Whidbey reported that of sixteen townships surveyed, six had burned-over forests. Furthermore, surveyors reported that Douglas fir was the dominant species, not the expected climax forest species of cedar and hemlock. That could only have occurred with periodic fires which cleared the understory and gave the light-preferring Douglas fir seedlings an advantage over the shade-tolerant cedar and hemlock seedlings. And since thunderstorms and lightning strikes are rare occurrences in this region, the fires were probably set by humans—a practice that was continued by white settlers and loggers.

## The Shipwreck Legend

Not all past events are so readily traceable. One that remains a mystery is a legend that has circulated in Maxwelton for decades. The legend involves a shipwreck in the saltwater estuary, possible murder and the Snohomish natives. Several versions of the legend persist, and the story recurs in both native and white journals.

Cheif William Shelton

Local lore is that when plowing his land near the mouth of Maxwelton Creek, Leon Burley occasionally hit pieces of wood that appeared to be part of an old boat of some kind. John Williamson, who farms the old Everett Green place next to Burley's, reports, "Leon told me that from time to time he and his dad ran into old pieces of a boat when they were plowing. Leon said he put pieces of cleat and chain that he found up in one of his old barns."

On the other hand, Bill Steiner, a neighbor and longtime friend who often worked side by side with Burley, doesn't recollect Leon talking about a boat. "He talked about picking up rocks from his field and occasionally finding arrowheads. And he talked about coming upon piles of old shells that native folks had obviously left, but I don't remember him talking about a buried boat of any kind."

The full story appears in native history in *Our Totem Maker*, an unpublished manuscript written by Herbert C. Fish and Salish chief William Shelton (Wah-cah-dub) in the 1920s. Fish, the grandfather of John Williamson's wife Becky Green Williamson, was then a professor of history at the Normal School in Ellensburg. He began collaborating with Chief Shelton on a book of Shelton's life as a renowned totem pole maker.

When Fish died in 1936, Chief Shelton decided not to finish the book out of respect for his friend. Fish's daughter, Virginia Tozer of Ellensburg, granted permission to quote the still unpublished manuscript:

*Whidbey Island has a history going back three hundred years into the Spanish days. The Indians of long ago had a story that at one time a Spanish ship came into a harbor in the southeastern part of Whidbey for masts. The ship had on board a number of bulls, which they used for hauling the masts to the ship. Many times the Spanish played games and had bullfights on the flats along the shores. The Indians watched this scene from the hills, and they were filled with wonderment at the actions of these strange people. After a while, they decided that these were not gods but were human beings like themselves.*

*Early one morning they rushed the Spanish camp and killed all the men. They feasted on the bulls and stripped all the metal from the ship. The ship lay in the harbor generation after generation until it rotted away. The people of Maxwelton still pick up pieces of the old boat as they farm the field where the tragedy occurred so many years ago.*[3]

*Is there a shipwreck in Maxwelton's past?*

Another version of the story comes from Dorothy Neil's *By Canoe and Sailing Ship They Came.*[4]

In this account, which Neil took from a 1960 article by South Whidbey writer and historian Cora Cook, Joseph Whidbey of Captain George Vancouver's crew explored a small creek entering the east side of the bay near Maxwelton between July 2 and 4, 1792. The men rowed up the creek with a sandbar on their right and a bluff on their left. They found a shipwreck half submerged. Apparently even then it was obvious the ship had been there for some time.

She says rediscovery of the wreck was made in 1859 by Thomas Johns and Edward Oliver, the first white settlers of Deer Lagoon to the north of Maxwelton, who also claimed to have found wild oxen roaming among the trees.

Yet another version of the story comes from an undated newspaper article from the collection of longtime resident Myron Brixner. According to the article, Sid Nourse (another longtime resident) met with members of the Cannon Hunters Association of Seattle who had come out to learn more about the old buried ship in Maxwelton. The article speculated on whether the legendary shipwreck might have been a ship called the Blue Wing that set sail from Seattle and was never heard from again. It goes on to say:

> *There are other stories that the Indians attacked the ship out in the bay. It was crippled, and the crew drifted with the ship into the then much larger Maxwelton Creek. They never sailed it again and some of the pioneer families' children have told me how they played on the hull when they were children, always wondering about the fate of the marooned crew.*

There are obvious discrepancies in the stories. If the natives did indeed feast on the bulls, how was it that Johns and Oliver later found wild oxen roaming the area?

And Chief Shelton's memory specifically speaks of a harbor in the southeastern part of Whidbey–Maxwelton is southwest. If the ship was "in the harbor," how did the wreck get clear up on Burley's land?

Also surprising in Shelton's account is the killing of the Spaniards. Generally the Snohomish were a peaceful people.

However, what is impressive is the number of places the legend occurs. Perhaps a look at the history of early white explorers in this area will shed more light on the legend of the Maxwelton shipwreck.

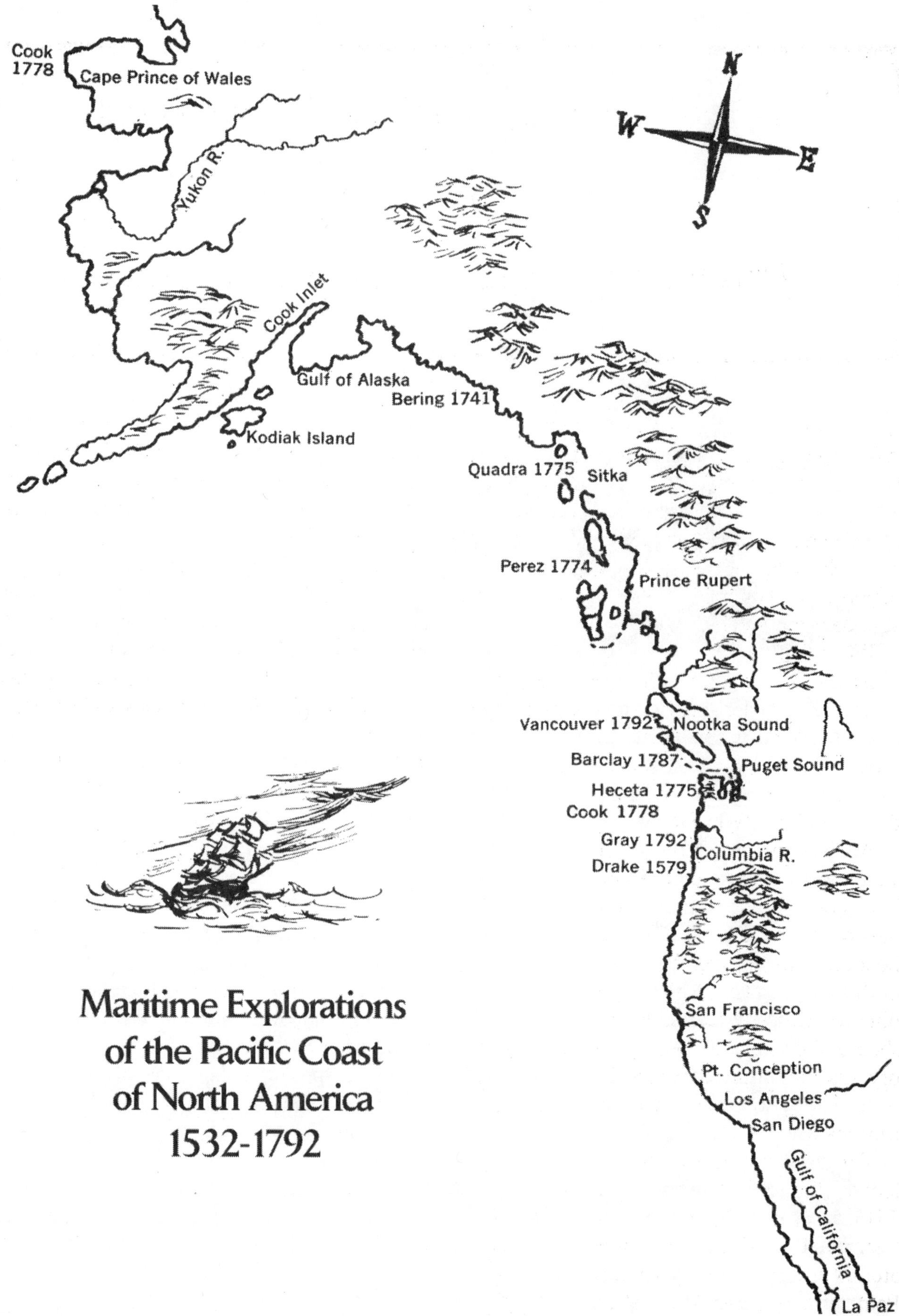
Maritime Explorations of the Pacific Coast of North America 1532-1792
N
W
E
S
Cook 1778
Cape Prince of Wales
Yukon R.
Cook Inlet
Gulf of Alaska
Bering 1741
Kodiak Island
Quadra 1775
Sitka
Perez 1774
Prince Rupert
Vancouver 1792
Nootka Sound
Barclay 1787
Puget Sound
Heceta 1775
Cook 1778
Gray 1792
Columbia R.
Drake 1579
San Francisco
Pt. Conception
Los Angeles
San Diego
Gulf of California
La Paz

A Journey Through the Maxwelton Watershed

Chapter 2

# Uncharted Waters ~ Early Explorers

It is 1513. Spanish explorer Vasco Nunez de Balboa is in search of a passage from the Atlantic Ocean to the riches of the Orient. Yet the Snohomish tribe of the Salish, living on the south end of Whidbey Island, already have all the great riches that a land-based people can imagine—a region blessed by mild climate, lush forests and abundant marine life.

While Balboa is risking his life to sail in uncharted waters in a ship that is perilously small by modern standards, his native counterparts in the Maxwelton watershed are busy gathering berries or fishing for salmon in the marshy creek that flows into Puget Sound.

At that time the Maxwelton watershed wasn't charted either, but its boundaries were well understood by a people who depended on fresh water. Members of the village at Cultus Bay likely discovered this extensive watershed to the northwest during the dry summer months when the water source for their own encampment dried up.

The Maxwelton watershed looked considerably different in 1513 than it does today. The Snohomish paddling their canoes around Scatchet Head and Indian Point would enter Maxwelton Creek between a long sand spit and the cliffs on the north side of the creek's entrance into Useless Bay. The saltwater estuary they entered would have extended as far as present day French and Bailey roads.

During ebb tide, the area drained out and exposed mudflats much like those in the Lake Hancock estuary of central Whidbey Island. In place of today's cattails, farm fields and reed canary grass, the estuary then supported salt-tolerant plants such as bulrushes and sedges.

*The sand spit as it appeared in an 1872 map.*

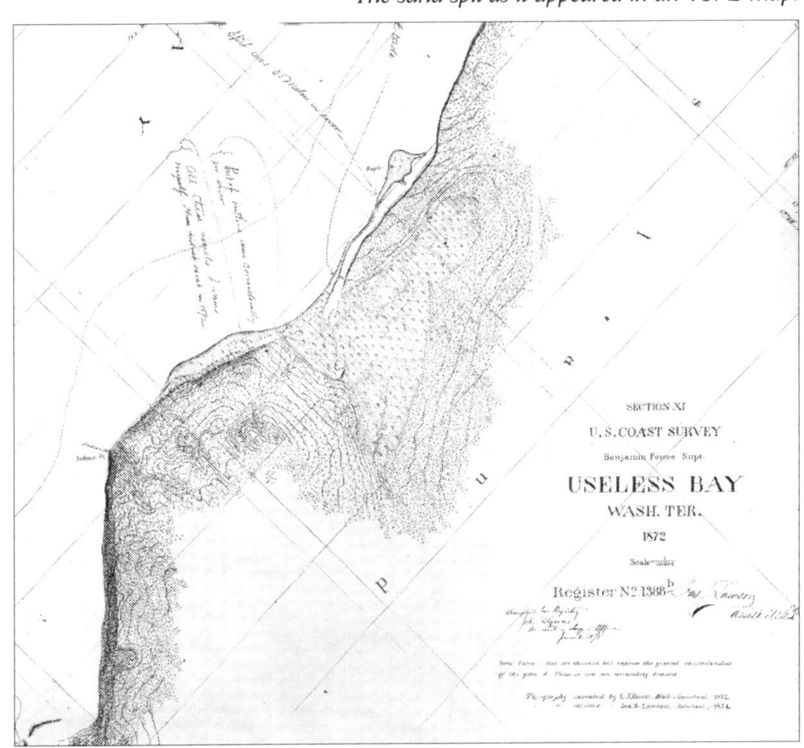

The early upper watershed was marked by dense stands of old-growth Douglas fir, hemlock and cedar. Today it holds farm fields, residential dwellings and second and third-growth timber.

There were primarily two species of salmon that populated the creek: coho (or silver), which spend two years maturing in the upper tributaries of the creek before entering Puget Sound; and chum, which spend a matter of months maturing in the saltwater estuary before entering Puget Sound. Searun cutthroat trout also shared the creek.

At the time Balboa was laying claim to the Pacific Ocean for Spain, the creeks and rivers of the Northwest were alive with the great salmon runs. In the fall, creeks like Maxwelton were choked with salmon two, three and even four layers thick struggling to come back and reach the precious gravel bars that could hold their eggs. No obstacle was big enough to thwart the drive to carry on their genetic lineage. And though wading bears were swatting them, eagles were snaring them in the shallows and the Snohomish were spearing them from the shore—still they came in numbers so great it defied human understanding.

## The Northwest Passage

Into this ecosystem that was providing an ample living for native peoples, came the Europeans looking for a passage to the riches of China. They were not looking for salmon or timber or fur. These early explorers were looking for a quicker way to get the silk, pearls, tea, and spices of the Orient than the difficult land route through Turkey and Afghanistan.

It was commonly believed by all the seafaring European nations—once they were convinced the world was round—that the first one to find a sea route for transporting treasures from the Orient to Europe would seed an empire. It took several decades for them to notice that the natural resources of this remote area were far more valuable than a route to the Far East.

While Balboa did not discover the fabled Northwest Passage in 1513, he did glimpse the Pacific Ocean and claimed for Spain all lands whose tributaries emptied into this vast sea. It was a grandiose claim that the British, the Russians, and eventually the Americans would challenge.

*Vasco Nunez de Balboa claimed the world's largest watershed for one of the world's smallest countries. He called the Pacific Ocean the "South Sea."*

At first, Spain was occupied with conquering Central America and Mexico and fighting the Dutch, French, Portuguese and English. It was not until Spain received word that Russia's explorer Vitus Bering had crossed over the Bering Sea into Alaska in 1741 that the Spanish turned their eyes toward the Pacific Northwest.

In 1774 Juan Perez searched the Queen Charlotte Islands for Russians and their ships. A year later Bruno de Heceta and Juan Francisco de la Bodega y Quadra sailed as far north as Vancouver Island. Heceta's men were believed to be the first Europeans to set foot in what is now the state of Washington—near Cape Flattery.

Although white men still had not reached Puget Sound, native peoples were capable of canoeing hundreds of miles and had communication with nearby tribes. Word of the arrival of "men with no color" most certainly was spreading along the entire Northwest coast. And with Captain James Cook's voyage to the Northwest in 1778, word of the rich fur trade was rapidly spreading back to Europe and to the newly-formed United States of America.

### Vancouver's Exploration

In 1792 the English sent Captain George Vancouver to prove the existence of the Northwest Passage and to settle land disputes with Spain. From May 2 to June 11, 1792, Vancouver and his crew on the *Discovery* charted and explored bays, harbors and islands from south Puget Sound to Nootka Bay, Vancouver Island.

*Captain George Vancouver*

The accuracy of their mapping has astounded many historians. Some fifty years later, an American naval expedition led by Lt. Charles Wilkes found few errors in Vancouver's maps. Vancouver also kept detailed journals about his discoveries.

His journals provide some clues about the shipwreck legend. According to Vancouver's entries, he was not near Whidbey Island in early July 1792, as was reported in *By Canoe and Sailing Ship They Came.* He was actually hundreds of miles north. He does not mention a shipwreck or any exploration of a creek on the south end when he was near Whidbey.

A May 23, 1792 journal entry by Broughton (Vancouver's naturalist) relates a mooring near Double Bluff. And an early June entry in crew member Lt. Peter Puget's journal reports a circumnavigation of Whidbey Island and a rather graphic description of an encounter with a skunk. But neither Vancouver's nor any of his staff's journals validate the claim that members of his expedition rowed up an inland creek on any part of Whidbey Island.

However, a close look at Vancouver's journals does verify the presence of Spaniards in the area prior to his arrival. In June 1792 he describes finding the ships *Sutil* and *Mexicanna* moored at Birch Bay south of the present community of Blaine, Washington. Vancouver learned that these Spaniards were in their second year of exploring the Northwest coast.

He and Lt. Puget were welcomed aboard the *Sutil,* described as being scarcely bigger than the *Discovery's* launch boat. The Spanish ships traveled with Vancouver for a month to assist with mapping. At the end of the month the Spanish went their way, probably grateful to stop traveling with these mad Englishmen who insisted on rising at dawn and never stopping for siestas.

The information about the *Sutil* and the *Mexicanna* is significant to Chief Shelton's version of the story of the Maxwelton shipwreck. Spanish ships clearly were in the vicinity of Maxwelton in the late 1700s and these ships were small enough that they could have entered a creek with no more than five or six

feet of draft. It is possible that a small Spanish ship the size of a British launch could have made its way up as far as Leon Burley's future field.

## Claiming the Northwest

By the 1790s, the attention of explorers in the Pacific Northwest was shifting away from finding a route to the Orient to harvesting the resources of the area. And the first resource that they focused on was animal furs, particularly the lush pelts of sea otters. Explorers found they could trade a few metal trinkets with natives for a sea otter pelt that would sell in the Orient for $100. The Russians led this chase for sea otter furs. By 1804 they had defeated the Tlingit tribes for control of Sitka and established a lucrative northern fur trade with the Orient.

By 1821 the British Hudson's Bay Company dominated the southern region commercially, but the young United States was not ready to hand over the Northwest to England. Robert Gray's voyage of 1792, Lewis and Clark's 1805 expedition up the Missouri River to the Pacific Ocean, the founding of Astoria in 1811, and Lt. Wilkes' survey and mapping expedition to Puget Sound in 1841 all represent early U.S. claims to the Northwest.

*The Hudson's Bay Company crest reflects their trade in furs.*

In the first half of the 1800s a number of treaties were signed which established the boundaries of the four Euro-American powers in the Pacific Northwest. Spain relinquished its claims in 1819. The Russians signed the famous 54'40° treaty in 1824. In 1846, after decades of negotiation with the British, the Oregon Territory up to the 49th parallel became part of the United States. The Hudson's Bay Company was allowed to continue trading in the territory.

During that same fifty years, native peoples were experiencing huge changes. Their initial exposure to white culture was largely through the fur trade. In return for furs the natives were given traps, tobacco, wine and even guns. Through this contact they also contracted smallpox, tuberculosis, measles and syphilis. Estimates in 1774 put the native population on the Northwest coast at about 188,000. In one hundred years their numbers had dwindled to 38,000.[5]

Even before the coming of white settlers, the people of the canoe were losing their way of life.

## Chief Patkainum

Historian Edmond S. Meany described in detail one native leader who rose up to take a stand against the influx of outsiders.[6]

He noted that in response to Thomas W. Glasgow's 1848 claim of land on Whidbey Island, Patkainum, chief of the Snoqualmie and Snohomish, called a council of all Puget Sound tribes.

To prepare for the important gathering on Whidbey Island, Chief Patkainum had his men construct a gigantic corral with wings that extended across the island from Penn Cove to Glasgow's claim near Ebey's Landing. Using dogs and brush beaters, more than sixty deer were rounded up and killed for a great intertribal banquet.

Patkainum gave a speech saying that if the whites were allowed to settle, native people would be taken away in "fire ships" (steamers) to distant lands where they'd perish. He argued for death to the newcomers so that native peoples could remain in possession of their lands.

His speech did not sit well with many of the tribes in the upper Sound region, quite possibly including the Snohomish from the South Whidbey longhouses. Even without gaining full support, Patkainum and his followers proceeded down to Ft. Nisqually near Tacoma and attacked troops stationed there.

Following his defeat and a trip to San Francisco where he was impressed by the magnitude of white settlement, Patkainum completely reversed his stand on the prospect of settlers. In a poignant speech, he picked up a handful of sand, letting the grains sift through his fingers. He told his people that the number of white people coming was greater than the grains of sand on a beach and that cooperation was the only way to survive their arrival.

On January 22, 1855 Patkainum signed a treaty ceding to the United States all lands from Elliott Bay north to the British line, including Whidbey Island. He then served as a captain in the U.S. Army during the Indian War of 1856. Many years later—on July 26, 1922—the city of Everett recognized his contributions by erecting an eighty-foot totem pole in his honor. Chief William Shelton (Wha-cah-dub), the author and talented Snohomish Indian of Tulalip, carved the pole.

## The Maxwelton Shipwreck

*"A legend is an unverifiable story handed down by tradition from earlier times and is popularly accepted as historical."*

Random House Unabridged Dictionary

One of the most careful keepers of records during the exploration of the Pacific Northwest was Captain George Vancouver. However, neither his logs nor any of his officers' journals mention seeing a shipwreck in any area of Whidbey Island. His logs do show that Spaniards aboard the tiny ships *Sutil* and *Mexicanna* were exploring the Northwest region as early as 1791.

This lends support to Chief Shelton's story about a Spanish ship coming into a South Whidbey harbor for masts. And Patkainum's story shows that Salish people were sometimes hostile to whites—as Chief Shelton's story indicates.

The legend of the Maxwelton shipwreck has several elements of historical truth. Yet, because of the lack of recorded information, many "facts" can never be checked—the age, size, name and exact location of the shipwreck—and so it must remain part of the unverified lore of Maxwelton.

A Journey Through the Maxwelton Watershed

Chapter 3

# Live Water ~ The First Settlers

An explorer studies and investigates new areas and then moves on to the next uncharted place. Because the early Maxwelton area confronted the Euro-American explorers with immense forests, dense underbrush, wild animals and high hills, they apparently did not investigate the lands beyond the shoreline—except possibly to look for fresh water or timber to repair masts, as in the shipwreck legend.

A settler comes to establish residence and figure out how to make a living from the land. People settle where they can find life's basic necessities: food and water. "If you're going to buy a place, make sure it has live water on it," says Midvale farmer Roy Hagglund.

Twenty-six-year-old Virginian Robert Bailey arrived in 1850 as the first non-native settler on the south end of Whidbey Island. He found land with "live" water on it because he settled near the native village of Digwadsh at the head of Cultus Bay. Virtually all native villages were near a water source.

Digwadsh was a potlatch center for the entire Snohomish tribe and contained six or seven longhouses. Bailey came to set up a trading business with the Snohomish. On September 1, 1852 he became the first recorded white landowner on South Whidbey by filing claim on 82.5 acres of land near the village. Shortly thereafter he married a local woman. The introduction of settlers to South Whidbey began as early western settlement often did–an adventuresome bachelor finds a local wife, and their children bridge the different worlds of the father and the mother.

White settlement in the lands of the Maxwelton watershed did not begin for another

*Many pioneer families, like the P. H. Mackies, stayed in the area for generations.*

**Some of the Early Settlers in Maxwelton Watershed**
(with apologies to those not documented)

**1852**—Robert Bailey files claim on Cultus Bay land and becomes the first recorded white landowner on South Whidbey.

**1863**—Luther Moore purchases 800 acres in the lower Maxwelton area.

**1870**—Ellen Lyons buys land from Moore. Son Michael Lyons and his wife Mary move to Whidbey and start logging. Mary is first known white woman to live on S. Whidbey.

**1880**—Jacob Anthes arrives at Quinn homestead (claim date unknown but described as "one of the first homesteads" on South Whidbey).

**1882**—Dr. P. B. Miller buys land in upper watershed around the lake that is now named for him. A mill was later located north of the lake.

**Late '80s**—John and Nellie Parsons acquire the Quinn homestead and turn it into a thriving farm.

**1889**—Herman Kyllonen homesteads 160 acres on a hill (present location of Campbell Road) for logging and then farming.

**1902**—Charles E. Feek buys Dr. Miller's logged-over 600 acres and begins farming in the upper watershed.

**1902-03**—Warren Wildes moves to Whidbey; owns and logs 600 acres in upper watershed with Louis Cuthbertson.

**1903**—Herman and Sara Kinskie buy 20 acres from John Parsons for a farm.

**1904**—John A. Brixner comes to help build Feek's house, and stays.

**1905**—Mackie Brothers purchase 900 acres in lower watershed (the Moore-Lyons land) and name the area Maxwelton.

**1909**—J. A. Brixner, the Mackies, Feek and others begin dividing their land to sell and increase the Maxwelton population.

twenty years, though it is certainly possible that Bailey and/or his children did some exploring of the area while hunting or gathering berries. The next settlements close to the watershed were established at Double Bluff and Deer Lagoon by William T. Johnson, Edward Oliver and Thomas John Johns.

The Maxwelton area took a step toward settlement in 1863 when Luther Moore filed a claim on 800 acres. His patent, as it was called, was signed by Abraham Lincoln. Little is known of Moore other than that he, like many in his day, bought and sold land as an investment. When he sold a portion of his land to Ellen Lyons in 1870, the necessary ingredients for the first settlement in the Maxwelton watershed were in place—a landowner with a resource and a market for that resource.

Ellen and her son Michael Lyons owned and operated the Lyons Hotel at Port Ludlow. Port Ludlow also had a sawmill, operated by the Phinneys. Thus the Lyons had a ready-made outlet for any timber they would cut on their property and the Phinneys had a way to get at the big timber of South Whidbey.

Shortly after Ellen purchased the land, Michael and his wife Mary started a logging operation and established a home overlooking the salt marsh. Mary was the first white woman to live on South Whidbey.

Like Oliver and Johns in Deer Lagoon, the Lyons logged using yoked oxen and skid roads to bring the cut trees from the woods to the beach. Logs were then floated into huge rafts and pulled by tugboat to the mill in Port Ludlow. From there lumber was often sent to San Francisco aboard ships based in Port Townsend.

Records show that in 1879 the Lyons sold 250 acres of their property to F. W. James of Port Townsend for $600 in gold coins.[7] Six years later Edward Oliver sold James 164.4 acres of his land farther north. Perhaps the prime timber close to the water had been cut, leading these small logging operations to sell off land to help pay their bills.

Little other recorded information is available about white settlers in the Maxwelton area prior to the 1900s except for a letter written by Jacob Anthes to Coupeville historian George Kellogg in 1910 about his experiences decades earlier.

## A Wilderness Journal

When Jacob Anthes arrived on the shores of South Whidbey in 1880, he was a boy of fifteen and eager for new experiences.

As he told the story, the German-born Anthes had gradually made his way across the young United States and met a man named Pat Quinn who was the headwaiter at the old Occidental Hotel in Seattle. Quinn had a homestead on Whidbey Island he was willing to pay Anthes $1.50 a day to "hold down." A logger named Christopher Anderson of Stetson Post's Useless Bay Camp was to show young Anthes the land, which was three miles from his camp.

*After the skiff deposited us on the island, we stopped at the old Mike Lyons' place where Maxwelton is located today. We followed what Mr. Anderson called a trail, covered with logs and brush, which showed there had been very little travel over it. In about an hour we arrived at what he called the farm. A shack about ten by twelve feet, covered by trees and ferns, was to be my home. I fail to see to this day what possessed that man Quinn in filing on a place in such a wilderness. This was one of the first homesteads filed upon on the south end of Whidbey.*[8]

*Jacob Anthes was responsible for founding the city of Langley, but first he explored the Maxwelton watershed.*

Anthes went on to describe the abundance of water and wildlife near the homestead.

*In passing a slough on the trip to the place, I noticed the water was alive with salmon as far as the eye could reach which I would not have believed had I been told of it without seeing it for myself, and the saltwater marsh seemed alive with geese and ducks, hardly paying any attention or showing any fear.*

For three weeks he saw no one and tended the homestead by doing things like clearing a three-quarter-mile trail to the beach. Then two men and a woman arrived with a letter from Mr. Quinn requesting that Anthes give possession

of the place to them.

Anthes was eventually paid his promised fee and he said that "this place changed hands a number of times until John Parsons stuck to it and made it one of the best ranches on the south end of the island."

Anthes' description brings alive the world of 1880 in the lower Maxwelton watershed. Since the Lyons had established a logging camp a decade earlier, it would make sense that many of the large trees at the edge of the saltwater marsh were cut down. However, Anthes' description says nothing of cut trees. Rather, his focus is on the pristine wilderness in which he finds himself. So vast was the wilderness of the early watershed that a single decade-long hand logging operation seems to have made very little visual impact.

Anthes was obviously enormously impressed with the abundance of wildlife, particularly salmon, during his three-week fall adventure on the Quinn homestead. Other than the scientific assumption that Maxwelton Creek should have had runs of chum and coho salmon, his is the first written record that such runs actually did occur. He was there in the fall and saw the

water alive with salmon answering the call to spawn. His description leaves little doubt that Maxwelton was at one time a prolific salmon creek and estuary.

Anthes was both an explorer and a settler of early South Whidbey. From this first introduction to the Maxwelton watershed he went on to explore, mostly on foot, all of South Whidbey. "In my wanderings I met all the settlers living on the south end of the island as far as Holmes Harbor, covering a distance of fifty miles." Yet the only settler he mentions in the Maxwelton watershed is Mike Lyons.

"I found that nearly all the ridges and high hills on this part of the island run in such a way that the place where Langley now stands could be reached without crossing any of them from any part of South Whidbey." And so his focus shifted to the east side of the island where he established early Langley as a settlement and a business center for the entire south end.

It would not be until 1905—when the Mackie brothers purchased 900 acres, basically those bought in 1863 by Luther Moore and later settled by Mike and Mary Lyons—that the Maxwelton area would draw enough attention to be truly settled.

So despite the fact that Washington's statehood in 1889 drew further attention to Whidbey Island, the Maxwelton watershed remained a wilderness with very few settlers, visited by the Snohomish gathering berries, harvesting wood or fishing. As the calendar turned to the 1900s, Maxwelton was the last remaining frontier on Whidbey Island.

*Upper right: The lower watershed was filled with trees before logging made it possible to build homes. This photo is of the Maxwelton beach area in the '30s.*

*Lower right: The Mackie brothers named Maxwelton in 1905 and encouraged people to settle here. From left to right: David Thomas, Peter Howard, Theodore Seaman, and James Herbert.*

*Kids playing at the bottom of the old log chute on the Silliman property.*

*Loggers stood on a "springboard" platform to cut the giant old-growth trees.*

A Journey Through the Maxwelton Watershed

Chapter 4

# Logging the Forests

The Maxwelton watershed is endowed with many resources—year-round streams, good soils, salmon, wildlife, and forests. Other than water, the one most readily visible to early settlers was the forests. And so it was this resource that they harvested first. Logging also had a lasting impact on settlement patterns in the watershed.

An old-growth Douglas fir tree is impressive. Deeply furrowed brown bark. A trunk that four or five men cannot quite stretch their arms around. A straight trunk reaching nearly one hundred feet before the first branch. To Michael Lyons, the earliest white settler in the area, felling one such tree represented days of work.

First, Lyons had to notch the bark and establish a springboard—a platform to work from—ten or more feet from the ground. The bases of these mammoth trees were thick and contained a lot of pitch, so loggers cut them above the springboard level.

Next Lyons had to chip away at the trunk with a double-bladed axe until the giant tree fell.

Moving the tree from the forest to the water was at least as arduous as felling it. A pair of men worked together with a crosscut saw (nicknamed a "Swede fiddle") and laboriously cut the four- or five-foot diameter trunk into pieces a bull team of oxen could pull. The oxen then pulled the log section along a skid road to the water.

The skid road was a corduroy track of smaller logs smeared with thick railroad grease. Once in the water, logs were towed in booms to the nearest mill—in Lyons' case, to Port Ludlow.

The Lyons' 1870 logging operation was a small camp that probably operated only in spring and summer. Chris Anderson and other loggers from the Stetson Post camp farther west on Useless Bay ran a larger and more long-lived operation than Lyons. They also worked in the upper portion of the Maxwelton watershed.

When Dr. P. B. Miller purchased the area around Miller Lake in 1882 from Chris Anderson, manager of the Stetson Post camp, he was purchasing logged-over lands in order to develop a farm. This pattern—loggers purchasing land, cutting the timber and then selling the land—would be the way that much of Maxwelton was settled.

*Swede Fiddle of Tern Kinskie*

When Henry Silliman purchased 10 acres along the Maxwelton bluff on the west side of the lower estuary in 1910 for a summer place, he found fruit trees, an old log chute and an old right of way. Bud Silliman, Henry's grandson, believes it is the remains of an ox-drawn railroad. The land had been owned in the 1890s by the Tacoma Mill Company, so it was part of the area's earliest logging history.

## Technological Improvements

In the 1880s loggers around the Pacific Northwest increased the speed of felling trees by using both crosscut saws and axes—instead of just axes. About that time, most logging camps also switched from using oxen to using horses to move the logs more quickly to the water. The first trees taken out of the valley were Douglas fir. By the 1880s some cedar was also cut, but until the turn of the century hemlock was considered worthless for timber.

One of the biggest changes in logging technology was the invention of the "steam donkey" in 1882 by John Dobeer. Horses were replaced by a small steam engine set on skids and attached to four or five winches. Loggers attached cables from these winches to choker chains on logs. The engine then reeled in the logs from as far as a mile away.

It took a while for the steam donkey to make its way to Maxwelton. According to lifelong

*The steam donkey helped Northwest loggers move large logs. It also made logging more dangerous.*

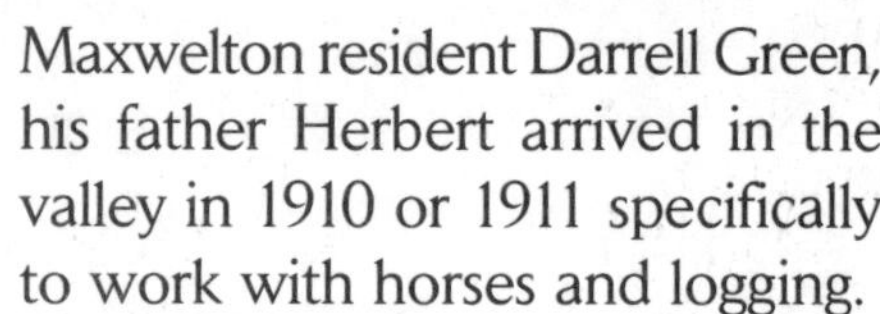

Maxwelton resident Darrell Green, his father Herbert arrived in the valley in 1910 or 1911 specifically to work with horses and logging.

"My great uncle Jones was working as a cook at a logging camp near Leon Burley's place. He knew my dad liked to work with horses so he wrote him a letter and suggested he come to work and have a chance to take care of a team of horses. Dad came in 1910 or 1911 and joined his uncle at the small logging camp."

"When Dad came here, they were logging the Maxwelton valley," continues Darrell. "The inland stuff was hard to get up on the hills. With horses you had to have a pretty near straight, flat shot down to the water. The Glendale railroad helped with the inland logging."

The Glendale railroad was built in 1905 and had about four miles of operating track at the height of its operation. Though the exact location of the entire line is not known, spur lines that entered the Maxwelton watershed can be found in the vicinity of French, Fiske, Bailey and Wildes roads.

The train was initially horse-drawn and carried one car at a time. Eventually a large trestle was built over Glendale Creek, and an engine was added.

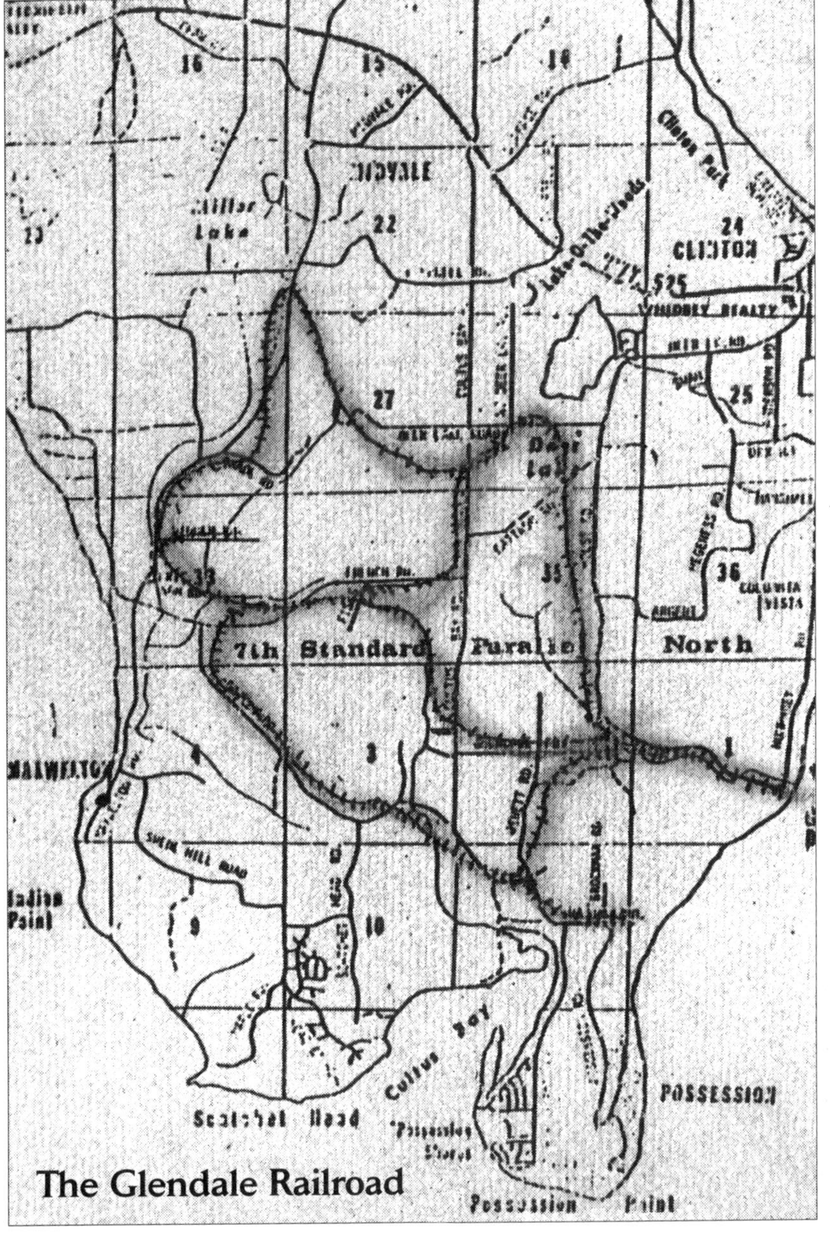

The Glendale Railroad

Little shacks appeared along the tracks to house workers. There could be as many as fifty people working on a "side"—brakemen, firemen, engineers, yarding crews, choker setters, hook tenders, chasers, cook, blacksmith. Workers earned about $2.50 a day and paid about $5 a month for housing.

## The Early Mills

According to Darrell Green, the first known mill in the Maxwelton watershed was built in the early 1900s north of Miller Lake. The next mill Green is aware of was a "gypsy mill"—a simple deck and saw without a roof—which his grandfather Peter Howard Mackie built where Swede Hill Road joins Maxwelton Road. The first use of that mill's lumber was in the 1910 construction of the buildings for the first Northwest Chautauqua gathering. It also provided the lumber to build the former Little Brown Church in about 1917.

The next mill at Maxwelton,

built sometime after 1910, was located at the mouth of Maxwelton Creek. Darrell Green remembers this mill. "I know my grandfather is the one who started it," he says. "I remember it as a shingle mill and a drying shed. I can still smell those bundles of cedar drying."

*The Evergreen Mill in the mid-1940s.*

## Maxwelton Loggers

*Warren Wildes* was born in Minnesota in 1876 and came to Maxwelton in 1902 or 1903. His daughter Margaret Wildes Seals recalls that her father and Louis Cuthbertson owned about 600 acres, which they logged together.

In 1906 Warren left the area and went to Vancouver Island to log. There he married Margaret Mills, a cook for the 250-man logging camp where he worked. Warren and Margaret remained in Canada until after World War I when they returned to Maxwelton. They raised nine children, two of whom, Parker and Lincoln, followed their father into logging. Margaret and Lincoln still live in the watershed.

*Lincoln Wildes* was born in 1926 and attended Intervale School with the Greens, Mackies, and Burleys. After service in the Marine Corps in World War II, he married Janice Burley in 1952 and worked as the head filer (sharpener of saws) at the island's Waterman Mill for 38 1/2 years before retiring.

*Parker Wildes* died in 1976 in a logging accident, killed by a "widow maker"—a limb or dead tree hanging in the canopy that a falling tree knocks down onto a logger. Parker was felling trees with a chainsaw and was alone at the time of the accident. Lincoln went to look for him when he didn't come home.

*Herbert Green* married Emily Mackie, daughter of one of the Maxwelton founders, in 1913. Sons Clay, Everett and Darrell all followed in their father's footsteps and chose careers that involved logging.

In the mid-1940s Herbert and his son *Everett* bought a small mill in the Bayview area and moved it to the site of the old Mackie shingle mill at the original outflow of Maxwelton Creek. They named the two-man operation Evergreen Mill and provided custom mill work until it closed in 1960. Everett then worked for the South Whidbey School District and as a handyman for many people in the Maxwelton valley. His daughter Becky now lives in the family house with her husband John Williamson.

*Darrell Green*, born in 1922, remembers hearing the steam donkey of his uncle *Clayton Howard Mackie*, the last son of Ada and Maxwelton founder Peter Howard Mackie. "When it started, it was so dang loud you wanted to be someplace else," says Darrell. He remembers that Clayton Howard logged Intervale Canyon (Quade Creek) in 1927 or 1928 using the first high lead logging on South Whidbey.

*Darrell Green*

In high lead logging, which started as early as 1910 in some places, loggers hung block or pulley atop a selected spar tree and ran a line through it from the donkey engine. This meant that logs could be moved through the air. Although this increased the speed by which they could be moved, it also increased the potential danger to which loggers were exposed.

Darrell worked as a timber faller with his uncle Clayton from 1940 to the early '50s, until Clayton moved to British Columbia to pursue a logging career. According to Peter Howard's son Seth, "The Classic U timber sale was junk compared to what he found up there. Being the youngest Mackie, he had inherited the farm but his career took him north." Seth, who was eight at the time, went on to a career in forestry.

"I remember Herb Green too," says Seth. "He was always chewing tobacco. He used to ask us kids if we wanted some of his 'brownie.'"

Seth also recalls that his uncle "Skid" Mackie got his nickname because he and some friends got caught pouring sand into the grease on the skid roads. When the loggers caught him, they rubbed the thick grease in his hair. "They had to shave his head to get it out."

Darrell bought part ownership in the Pioneer Mill at Bayview in the early 1950s. "At the time, there was no demand for logs," says Darrell. "But we found a market for them to the railroads—for crossarms, ties and such. We milled alder and some peeler blocks." Peeler blocks are any tree two feet in diameter and over. All veneer comes from peeler blocks.

Darrell moved the Pioneer Mill to Glendale in 1965 and employed seven or eight men. He sold the mill in 1970 and then spent his last working years as a postman for Clinton.

*Clay Green,* the oldest of Herbert's boys, eventually worked for the Waterman Mill until he retired in 1980. He was also a baseball player like his father, and at one time played on a semi-professional team in Oak Harbor.

*Clarence "Tern" Kinskie,* who came to the Maxwelton area in 1903 as a child, did not marry until he was forty-one. When he returned from World War I, he spent a lot of time living in logging camps as a faller. However once he and his wife Susan had children, he stayed closer to home.

His daughter Mary Sue Lile remembers that one of her father's jobs was blowing up stumps with dynamite. "We had dynamite in the basement," she recalls. "He blew out all the stumps for Wildes Road." In his later years Tern said, "I should have become a carpenter like my dad. No one ever thought the trees would all be gone. When I got back from the war, logging

*The Kinskie Barn, 1903*

was the big thing."

*Floyd Grubb* had a thirty-three-year career as a logger. Born in Langley in 1909, by the late 1920s he was earning $4 a day cutting virgin timber up Swede Hill with a crosscut saw and axe. The seven- and eight-foot diameter trees were cut into logs, gathered by a donkey engine and dropped through a chute down into the Sound. "Those logs would come whistling down the chute with a splash you could see for miles," said Grubb.[9]

*Floyd Grubb in 1982*

Floyd was married in 1941 to Olive Gaylard, whose family had come to Maxwelton in 1921. Her sister Susan married Tern Kinskie. Floyd and Tern eventually purchased a logging truck together. Floyd died in 2001 and Olive still lives in their French Road home.

## Fire and Other Dangers

Logging was a hazardous profession and stories abound about near misses. Tern Kinskie lost a leg. Twice Floyd Grubb nearly lost his life while working around high lead logging. In one instance he was standing next to his truck in a log yard watching a log come in, when it began to swing wildly and killed the man standing next to him—all in a matter of seconds.

Logging operations create piles of slash. During the bull team and horse-logging days, only easily transportable and highly desirable log sections were taken out of the woods. Since loggers assumed the supply of trees was endless, they often discarded everything above the first branches of the tree. This contributed to huge amounts of slash on the ground. It was not until the start of the shingle industry in the early 1900s that there was even a market, and therefore encouragement, for using smaller-diameter timber.

Though the piles of slash began to decrease in size in the 1900s because of more efficient usage, fire danger actually increased because there were more men in the woods and they began to use machines. Fires were frequent on lands that were being logged. Fires also regularly occurred on logged-over lands that were being stump-farmed.

"Back in the '20s we literally burned in order to farm amidst the stumps," says Ewing Road farmer Joe Long. "In the spring you'd set a match to burn the ferns and dead grass that had grown up between the stumps. Runaway fires were a problem."

In an August 12, 1925 letter to his brother, Henry Silliman described a time of serious fire near their property on Maxwelton Road. "All the men on the south end of Whidbey Island were fighting forest fires, but by Sunday [they] had back-fired around the most dangerous blaze near camp."

Now there is a Fire District #3 station at the corner of French and Bailey roads, but until well into the 1950s help had to come from as far away as Langley. The original Kinskie homestead burned to the ground in 1952 when fire trucks could not arrive quickly enough. Lumber from the Evergreen Mill and a community house-raising built the house now standing on the original homestead site.

The practice of burning stumps in the upper Maxwelton watershed ceased by the mid-1930s because the fires would travel down the roots of old stumps into the peat. Roy Hagglund described how the peat near his place in Midvale burned for several years before they could finally put it out by digging ditches over from Maxwelton Creek.

### Waterman Mill and Reforestation

Bud Waterman, who had been a logger since 1934, came to the island in 1948 and began buying up timberland in central and south Whidbey. According to his daughter Debra Waterman, "Timber didn't have status back then. It was easy to acquire land. There was little competition. Dad bought it, logged it and sold it." At one time Bud owned 3500 acres.

Because it was expensive to move logs to a mill, Waterman built his own mill on Langley Road in 1950. At the height of its operation the mill employed 16 people including Clay Green and Lincoln Wildes. Debra says that most of the logging being done at that time was second growth, though there still were some scattered pockets of old growth.

By the time it closed in 1991, on what the employees called "Black Monday," the mill was using most of what it cut. The mill sold all its sawdust and even marketed beauty bark for gardening. "We were able to use about 97 to 98 percent of a log," explains Debra. "The rest we burned in the wigwam burner." The mill sold mostly green framing material—about 70 percent of which was Douglas fir.

*The old wigwam burner still stands on the Waterman Mill site on Langley Road.*

Until 1975 there was no replanting of logged lands. In keeping with the tradition that the highest and best use for land was farming, logged lands were sold to prospective small landowners. However, by 1975 the State Department of Natural Resources implemented a program calling for replanting within three years of cutting. At first the Waterman Mill had a forester on site to comply with the reforestation rules. However, within a few years all the planting was contracted out.

Increasing regulations came with increased population on the island. In 1984 Island County created its first comprehensive plan. A "forest zone" was established that allowed for one house per twenty acres. Anything zoned as forestland was taxed at a substantially lower rate. "The downside of the 1984 regulations was that it was easy for anyone to opt out of them," explains Debra. "Anyone who applied for a rezone basically got it."

The new Island County Comprehensive Plan of 2001 allows one dwelling per ten acres on land zoned as forest and, according to Debra, it appears to have some enforcement teeth in it.

Bud Waterman died in 1981 and Debra continued to operate the mill until 1991. "We cut a lot of timber in those later years, because we couldn't purchase off-site timber," explains Debra. "Almost all available timber was going to Japan, Korea and Russia. Loggers could make a lot more money selling their logs abroad."

The closing of the Waterman Mill marked the end of over a century of active logging in the Maxwelton watershed. Individual landowners are still doing small timber cuts, but basically logging is a dying profession in the area.

*View of lower Maxwelton Creek and the former saltmarsh/estuary.*

A creek, given its visual complexity, is a surprisingly simple construction.
Two nouns: Water and Land. One verb: Gravity.
Plants and animal life, growth and decay, the play of light on water,
the visual and liturgical improvisations of current, all obscure the simplicity.
But the grammar of creeks is the antithesis of complex. The instant it alights on Earth, the first noun—Water—is turned by the verb, Gravity, into a ceaseless search for the lowest possible place while the second noun, Land, does all in its passive power to thwart that search.
The result? Riffle; rapid; eddy; pool; scouring sand; sculptured wood and rock;
soil-making mud; insects; birds; fish; *ar-ka*; endless music; sustenance; life.

David James Duncan, in *My Story as Told By Water*

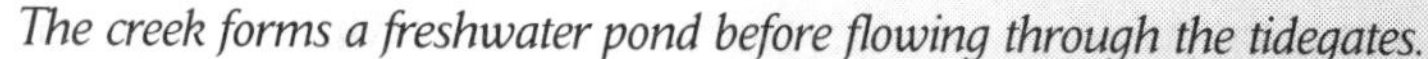

*The creek forms a freshwater pond before flowing through the tidegates.*

A Journey Through the Maxwelton Watershed

Chapter 5

# The Lower Watershed

Many people credit the growth of Maxwelton to the arrival of the charismatic Mackie brothers and their large families in 1905. As they learned to till the land, the Mackies joined hands with existing settlers to build homes and barns. They also took an active role in convincing people from Seattle to buy land and settle in this last frontier of Whidbey Island.

## Maxwelton Takes Shape

The Mackie clan left their Scottish homeland for Canada and then moved on to Nebraska in 1871. The four brothers continued to move west. Theodore made his way to Seattle and acquired some money operating three hotels there. He wrote his brothers, "I have found a beautiful section of land I think we could homestead."[10]

Theodore financed the purchase of 900 acres in the lower Maxwelton area. His brother Peter Howard arrived on Whidbey first. Theodore Seaman, James Herbert, and David Thomas followed. The brothers were often referred to by their first and middle names or initials alone.

Peter Howard's pregnant wife Ada and their eight children—twins Emily and Julia, Wallace, Hiram, James, Joseph, Florence and Donald—arrived in July 1905 with chickens, a cow and all their worldly possessions aboard the sternwheeler *Fairhaven.* Bossy the cow was pushed overboard to swim ashore and everything else was loaded aboard a barge to be floated in at high tide. P. H. and Ada would have four more children and would be instrumental in bringing another level of settlement to the area.

The Scottish folk song, "Annie Laurie," begins with the line "Maxwellton's braes [hills] are bonnie." The musical Mackie brothers are said

to have broken out singing this song when they saw the beauty of their new homeland. Within a very short time, their use of Maxwelton became the recognized name of this beautiful valley with its heavily forested hills.

*Welcoming people to the Maxwelton Chautauqua.*

Resupply for all the early settlers was difficult, as interior roads were sparse and at least initially there was no dock at the Maxwelton beach. The Mackies purchased a gasoline launch and made trips to Everett for 50-pound sacks of flour, sugar and other case-lot goods. Before the dock was built in about 1908, neighbors often relied on the Mackies for supplies and services—such as a ride to the doctor in Everett or Edmonds.

Births were another story, though. Ada delivered all of her children at home. Her daughter Florence would grow up to be a midwife to many valley births.

By June 1909 the aspirations of the Mackie brothers were showing up in print. Theodore S. Mackie ran this advertisement in the *Everett Herald*:

*The new town located on the south end of Whidby Island . . . If you want an ideal home or farm where you can raise an abundance of all kinds of crops, go to Maxwelton. It will without doubt be the largest town on the island in the near future, and is the coming summer resort of Puget Sound.*

Shortly thereafter, P. H. Mackie ran an ad for summer homes at Maxwelton. *Lots are valued as low as $100 and may be secured on payments of ten percent down and $1 per month per $100 of the purchase price. Opening prices on these lots are much lower than on any waterfront property of this class now on the market.*

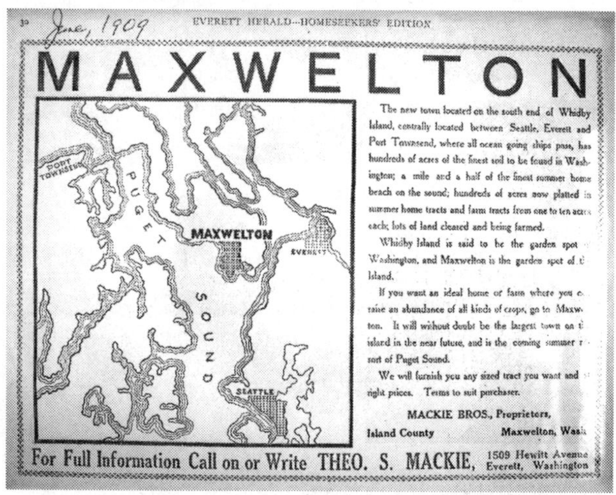

June, 1909 EVERETT HERALD—HOMESEEKERS' EDITION

MAXWELTON



The new town located on the south end of Whidby Island, centrally located between Seattle, Everett and Port Townsend, where all ocean going ships pass, has hundreds of acres of the finest soil to be found in Washington; a mile and a half of the finest summer home beach on the sound; hundreds of acres now platted in summer home tracts and farm tracts from one to ten acres each; lots of land cleared and being farmed.

Whidby Island is said to be the garden spot of Washington, and Maxwelton is the garden spot of the Island.

If you want an ideal home or farm where you can raise an abundance of all kinds of crops, go to Maxwelton. It will without doubt be the largest town on the island in the near future, and is the coming summer resort of Puget Sound.

We will furnish you any sized tract you want and right prices. Terms to suit purchaser.

MACKIE BROS., Proprietors,
Island County Maxwelton, Wash.

For Full Information Call on or Write THEO. S. MACKIE, 1509 Hewitt Avenue Everett, Washington

An article in the October 21, 1909 issue of the *Langley Islander* included the following comment about the desire for more settlement on Whidbey Island:

*Maxwelton is growing rapidly. One of the foremost incentives to this growth has been the division of several large properties into ten, twenty, thirty and forty acre tracts. J. A. Brixner was the first to start*

*this movement by putting 168 acres on the market in small tracts, and partially through his influence the Mackie Brothers have divided up some 500 or 600 acres; Norman Cuthbertson, 160 acres; and C. E. Feek, 400 acres... Anything that will help to populate the island and put its fertile lands under cultivation will be a help to every resident of the county in one way or another.*

## Festival Draws Settlers

Perhaps the greatest pull to bring newcomers to the area came from the first Northwest Chautauqua held in the summer of 1910.

The "Chautauqua"—pronounced sha-talk-wah—was a system of adult education that began in 1873 on the shores of Lake Chautauqua, New York. The festivals often combined Bible study and Sunday school classes with popular entertainment and lectures on history, science and art. The idea of summer religious study and general education grew and Chautauquas eventually spread as far as India and China, as well as all over the United States.

The Mackie brothers campaigned for a Chautauqua in the Northwest and succeeded in locating it at Maxwelton. They donated the land under the Swede Hill bluff for the Chautauqua grounds, and Peter Mackie supplied the lumber for the outdoor theater.[11]

Bleachers for the outdoor theater.

The program for the first Maxwelton Chautauqua, held for two weeks July 19 to 31, 1910, extols the beauty of its site. It speaks of "a bathing beach where a quarter mile of clean white sand is exposed at high tide." It goes on to describe a "forested bluff that provides a backdrop to a 3/4 mile-long strip where there are tenting spots and an amphitheater that will seat 4,000."

Entrance to the Chautauqua grounds.

The program does not mention the fact that this ambitious undertaking was going to be hosted by a community of only twenty families. In the roster of officers, directors and advisory board members, only Peter H. Mackie was listed with a Maxwelton address. J. J. Burley, Leon's father, was listed as the carpenter but his address, like that of the others, was still Seattle.

Featured speakers included the

charismatic evangelist Billy Sunday, Zint Kalla Nuni (an Indian girl), missionary Willis Hotchkiss, Dr. Sam Small and Judge Frank P. Sadler of Chicago. Music was provided by the Chautauqua Ladies' Orchestra and the Fort Casey Military Band.

The state health department approved the construction, and the Baptist Summer Assembly elected to hold its meetings on the grounds. The cost of a season ticket was $2; rental of an 8 x 10 tent was $2.50 for the entire two weeks.

The following summer there was some controversy about whether the Northwest Chautauqua would be held at Maxwelton or at Manitou Park on Bainbridge Island because it was closer to the population center of Seattle. But an article written by P. H. Mackie for the *Island County Times* on May 26, 1911 called for people in Island and Snohomish counties to pull together to make a "grand success" of the Maxwelton gathering. Mackie's advocacy worked, and once again the Northwest Chautauqua was held at Maxwelton.

Giant winter snows collapsed the roof of the amphitheater in 1916, and the Maxwelton Chautauqua was gone forever.

*The Chautauqua camping grounds as seen from the bluff above.*

## A Guiding Force

Grandchildren of P. H. Mackie living into the 21st century have fond memories of him and shed some light on why he was able to accomplish so much for his community. Seth Mackie, son of P. H.'s youngest son Clayton Howard, speaks about men coming from Seattle to seek Peter Howard's advice about the future of hydroelectric power. Myron Brixner, son of P. H.'s daughter Julia, says, "I idolized my grandfather. He was brilliant and well-read."

Seth chuckles when he shares a story about how his grandfather adjusted to changing times. He explains that his grandfather was one of the first people in the valley to get a car—a 1915 Buick. "As the story is told, grandpa drove it into the garage for the first time and said 'whoa!' However, the car didn't obey and drove right through the wall into the side of the hill. My dad told me that his sons proceeded to put a big bumper log at the back of the garage so they wouldn't have to rebuild it again."

Many remember Peter Howard as the tall, lanky redheaded man dressed up like Uncle Sam for the Fourth of July parades. The 1911 book *Island County, A World Beater* credits him with raising three tons of hay to the acre, earning $8 a month from his cows, and growing apples with a yield as high as twenty boxes per tree.

When asked how P. H. Mackie managed to raise twelve children, run a farm and a small saw mill, and help organize a Chautauqua, his grandson Darrell Green responded, "He had my grandmother and eight sons. Ada was a won-

derful, wonderful woman who was a great gardener. She had a lot of great sayings like, 'Choose your words. You might have to eat 'em.'"

Clair "Jack" Mackie, grandson of Theodore and son of Ivan, remembers going to the island as a boy in the 1920s. "In the early days we went by boat to the island, sixty cents from Seattle, big ham sandwiches for a quarter. Gramp would meet us according to directions on our card."

Clair explains that "there were no direct phone lines to the island—just a local hand crank party line to the beach—so Gramps sent a post card when he wanted to let folks know that it was time for a visit." Now a Freeland resident, Clair recalls his grandfather as a man who could fix almost anything and had a wonderful sense of humor.

## Farming Near the Saltwater Marsh

Farmers generally bring stability to an area. They tend to have large families. They exhibit a strong work ethic. And the nature of their work demands that they remain in place for a long time. The farmers who arrived in Maxwelton at the turn of the century did not generally arrive to rich and fertile lands. In many cases the land was of marginal quality and full of logged-over stumps. In all cases the land would require a lot of work to become productive.

*The Mackie clan gathers for a portrait. Julia Mackie Cross sits down front.*

The stumps were difficult to get rid of, and the acidic soils of these logged-over forests were often infertile to all but growing more trees. In the early twentieth century there was little understanding of soil science. As late as 1931 the State Director of Agriculture for Washington recommended that farmers choose land with big stumps, as it indicated greater fertility.[12]

Governments, chambers of commerce, timber industry managers and urban leaders all encouraged people to move to the country and do their patriotic duty to settle the land and provide food for the growing cities. Population figures indicate that the number of farms in Island County tripled between 1900 and 1920.[13]

The Maxwelton area grew significantly during this time. The farmers who arrived earliest chose the easiest land to farm—the lands just beyond the tidal marsh. They were close to water transportation, reasonably fertile and not as densely forested. These families left a lasting impact on the watershed and some of them remain here today. Here are stories of two such families.

### The Parsons Place

Though Jacob Anthes wondered "what possessed that man Quinn in filing on a place in such a wilderness," in reality Quinn had chosen his homestead site in Maxwelton wisely. When John and Nellie Parsons eventually acquired the property in the late 1800s, they turned the land into a thriving farm.

Located just above the high-water mark of the salt marsh, yet still in the "bottomland," their farm contained rich soil. In addition to vegetables and a few cattle, John Parsons grew flower bulbs of many kinds. Nellie, an artist, played a pump organ and had Sunday afternoon church services in her living room. "As a child, I was bored with the services," recalls Evelyn Hagstrom Varon. "But I remember admiring Mrs. Parsons' many paintings hanging on the wall."

The place remains a farm to this day, as the series of new owners continued the farming tradition.

### The Kinskies

In 1903, Herman and Sara Kinskie bought twenty acres of the Parsons land for $150. The Kinskies' granddaughter Mary Sue Lile, who still lives on the land, says, "My grandfather came from Prussian roots, possibly related to the czars, so he had to be secretive about his upbringing because people were killed for such connections. My grandmother was orphaned and raised by a Welsh woman, so in many ways our family tree really begins here in the valley."

Herman was determined that his family would not starve. The first thing he built was the barn, which is still standing by the side of French Road. The family lived in a small cabin on the Parsons place while Herman raised the barn and later built a house. He planted apple, cherry and filbert trees, many of which are still growing today. "My daddy told me stories about grandpa cutting hay with a hand scythe and then walking to the barn carrying it on a pitchfork one bundle at a time," said Mary Sue.

*Mary Sue Kinskie Lile*

Like most early settlers, Herman Kinskie had a variety of skills. He was an accomplished carpenter and helped build the former Little Brown Church on the corner of French and Maxwelton roads. He also built a fine wooden ship, the *Alice K*, which had been commissioned by folks willing to pay for a yew hull and oak ribs. Herman and Sara had three daughters and one son, Clarence.

Clarence "Tern" Kinskie was born in Michigan in 1895 before his family moved to Whidbey Island. After a Maxwelton childhood, he was drafted toward the end of World War I and served his country in France. He returned from the war carrying some dried beans a farmer had given him to plant on his family's French Road farm. Kinskie beans have made their way into many gardens in the valley.

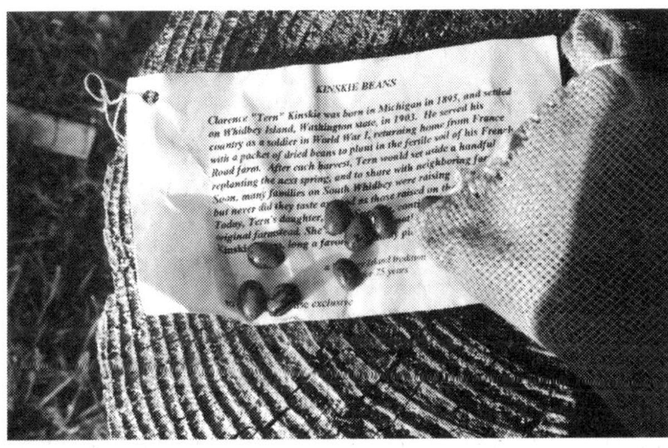


**Baked Kinskie Beans**

Soak 2 c. Kinskie Beans overnight in cold water.
Simmer in same water until tender (1-2 hrs).
Drain, reserving liquid.
Place in a 2 qt. beanpot, in layers:
- the drained beans
- 1/2 lb. bacon or salt pork
- whole slices of onion
- optional: sliced hot peppers

Combine and pour over layered beans:
- 3 Tbsp molasses — 1/2 tsp pepper
- 2 tsp Salt — 1/4 tsp dry mustard

Add enough bean liquid to just cover top layer.
Bake covered at 300 for 8 hrs. add more liquid or boiling water if beans seem dry. Serves 6.

Tern became a logger in the young community. Shortly after he started work, his leg got pinched between two logs and was improperly treated by a doctor. His leg had to be amputated, yet he worked a lifetime felling trees in the valley and far away.

Tern and Susan Gaylard Kinskie had a daughter Mary Sue and two sons, Art and Wilfred. Herman Kinskie died in 1928. Sara went on to outlive two more husbands before dying in 1961.

## Farming Above the Marsh

Not all the activity was on the flatlands of the marshes. The hills and ridges had their own pioneer families.

### Swede Hill

Morris Johnson, who owned many acres on the 360-foot hill at the south edge of the Maxwelton watershed, belonged to the Swedish Tabernacle in Seattle. There he recruited people to purchase tracts of his land. One of the early settlers to respond was David Hagstrom.

According to his daughter Evelyn Hagstrom Varon, Hagstrom built a two-story white house in 1911 atop what became called Swede Hill.

*The Hagstrom house atop Swede Hill Road.*

There he and his first wife Helen Melin raised four children. After Evelyn's father was widowed, he married Kathrine, a Norwegian immigrant. Evelyn was born a year later in 1921 and along with her family would become an integral part of pre-World War II island life.

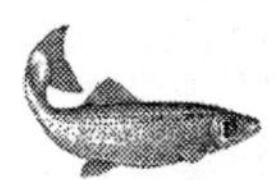



The Hagstroms are one of many families who exemplified the kind of hard work ethic that made it possible to live on the island in the days before electricity, paved roads and regular ferries.

Evelyn recalls the story of her mother ordering 500 baby chickens, moving furniture out of the dining room, covering the walls and installing a brooder in that part of the house. At the time her father was living on Queen Anne Hill in a "shack," working as a wood turner for Stetson Post. He commuted back and forth every two weeks on the steamers *Atlanta* or *Calista*.

By 1926 Kathrine Hagstrom had had enough of the lonely pioneer life and gave her husband an ultimatum—"I'm not going to stay out here all by myself." That was the year Jean was born and David moved back to the island full time.

### Prosperity Ridge

On July 30, 1906 Willard French purchased lands that had been homesteaded by Peter Nelson at the southeastern edge of the Maxwelton watershed, on what is now French Road.

This high area of the watershed, stretching lengthwise between French and Bailey roads, was dubbed "Poverty Ridge" until 1915 when Bruce and Viola Crawford bought twenty acres from the Frenches. Viola renamed it "Prosperity Ridge" when she wrote a local column for the *Oak Harbor Farm Journal.*

The Franklin and Arthur Fiske families settled on the ridge in 1908, just above the Kinskies. Franklin's daughter Amelia married Henry Bohnke who owned a 15-acre farm on the ridge on the other side of the valley. Part of his Sills Road farm later became Calvin's Conifers Tree Farm. Henry and Amelia's son Willis Bohnke, born in 1925, still remains on the island.

## Diking the Saltwater Marsh

The arrival of the Mackies, and their desire to expand settlement, raised the question of whether areas could be farmed that were flooded with salt water during high tides. By the early 1900s building dikes to block the flow of salt water and claim marshlands for farming was a common phenomenon in the Northwest. Such experiments in land management supported the general belief system of the time that farming was the highest and best use for any land.

On August 6, 1914 the Island County Commissioners ordered the creation of Diking District #2 to "construct a proper dike such that said land will not be subject to overflow and will become highly productive and that the value thereof will be very materially increased."[14]

*The 1915 map of the dike around the Maxwelton marsh.*

The new district contained 300 acres belonging to the Mackies, Montgomerys, Chapins, Thompsens, Waldrons, Mungers, Brixners, DeLongs, Sillimans and Pattons. On September 15, 1914 three commissioners were elected to direct the new district: G.G. Waldron, F.L. DeLong and D.T. Mackie. Assessments were collected to fund capital improvements, which included dikes and a tidegate.[15]

## The Summer People

Since the earliest days on Whidbey Island, there have been "summer people." These folks own property, often with simple amenities such as tent sites and outhouses, and come up during the summer when children are out of school and on weekends throughout the year. Many of them have established three- and even four-generation visitation loyalty to the Maxwelton watershed.

The Silliman cabin originally had a canvas roof.

The cabin today.

The Silliman family has been coming to

The Silliman and Patton families enjoy a summer meal.

Maxwelton for five generations. Henry D. Silliman, an engineer who designed Honolulu's first sewer system, arrived in 1910 as a guest of John DeWitt Patton, Sr. Patton was a draftsman who had worked for the city of Ballard and then Seattle, and had professional connections with Silliman. The same year, Silliman purchased ten acres from Patton along the Maxwelton bluff.

Another co-worker, civil engineer Charles E. McCrath, also purchased bluff property from Patton. Though he never established a residence on the island, McCrath is noteworthy for creating the 1915 Diking District #2 survey map.

Henry D. Silliman

The Silliman property is full of history. Apple trees that were planted in the late 1800s to feed the loggers are

still thriving. A log chute from the top of the bluff down to the beach is still visible. And the remnants of an ox-drawn railroad for moving logs signals the history of the land this family continues to honor and protect.

"We believe our property was logged in the 1880s by its previous owners," explains Bud Silliman, grandson of Henry. "We found hand-forged nails on the property and plenty of evidence that there was a cookhouse here to serve the loggers."

Bud and his brother Clark describe coming out for the summer even during World War II when there was gas rationing. "As soon as we arrived, we went to the Patton farm," says Clark. "We worshipped John Jr. He didn't have kids so we were like his surrogate kids. We played in the hayloft, got kittens, and ate apples. We just loved being there."

*Ellen McDonald's cabin on the beach.*

Another summer family tradition started in 1914 when Ellen McDonald and her husband Henry bought one of the Mackie beach lots. Henry arrived first and constructed a simple cabin.

Ellen and eight-year-old Eunice came out on a steamer some weeks later and arrived after dark. Since it was too dark to see anything, they simply slept on the beach until daybreak. That was the kind of flexibility it would take for Ellen to survive in this rural area.

Henry had a stroke in the early 1920s leaving Ellen—without electricity or plumbing—to care for an ailing husband and young daughter. Using her meager savings and an ability to harvest clams and other seafood, Ellen managed to raise Eunice after Henry died. Eunice married in 1937 and moved to Seattle, but remained close to her mother and to Maxwelton.

"We came out here on July 4 and stayed until September," says Diane McDonald Tinker, Eunice's daughter. "I can remember grandma bathing in the Sound in her woolen bathing suit until the 1950s. [Born in Norway in 1868, Ellen was well into her '90s at the time.] She was good friends with Evelyn Varon's mother because they both spoke Norwegian."

*Eunice McDonald on the porch of the cabin.*

Diane also remembers running barefoot "just like the local kids" all summer. "My shoes never fit in September because of the calluses on my feet," she said. Diane and her grown kids are still coming to the renovated old place.

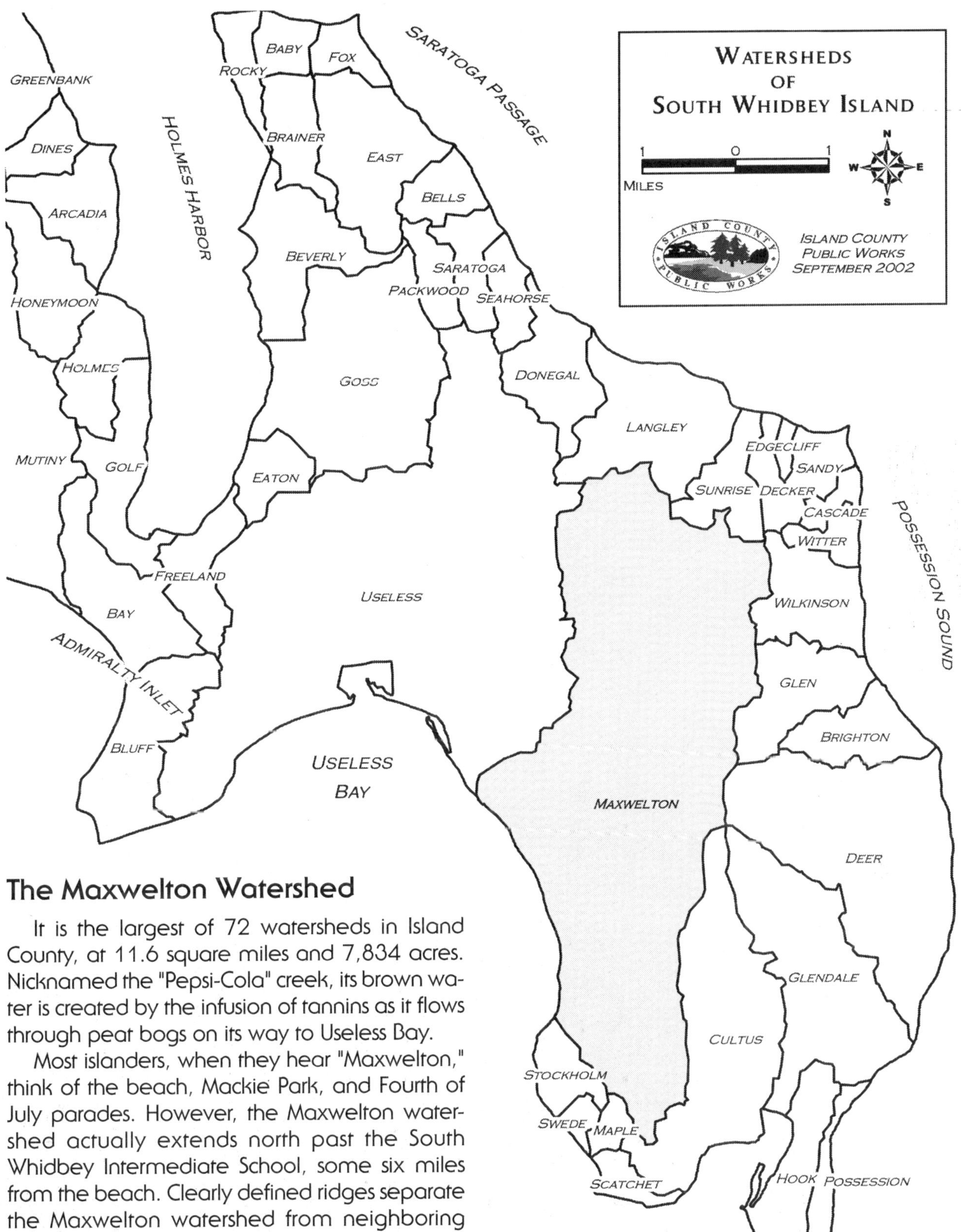


## The Maxwelton Watershed

It is the largest of 72 watersheds in Island County, at 11.6 square miles and 7,834 acres. Nicknamed the "Pepsi-Cola" creek, its brown water is created by the infusion of tannins as it flows through peat bogs on its way to Useless Bay.

Most islanders, when they hear "Maxwelton," think of the beach, Mackie Park, and Fourth of July parades. However, the Maxwelton watershed actually extends north past the South Whidbey Intermediate School, some six miles from the beach. Clearly defined ridges separate the Maxwelton watershed from neighboring Cultus watershed to the east and Useless watershed to the west.

Maxwelton Creek and its tributaries, such as Quade Creek, drain the Maxwelton watershed from the headwaters to Puget Sound through over 12 miles of stream.

Rainfall: 25-30" per year
Known fish use:
Coho, chum and sea-run cutthroat trout

*The 1903 Maxwelton School, above. The first Maxwelton store was located at the end of the dock built by the Mackies.*

A Journey Through the Maxwelton Watershed

Chapter 6

# Community Life

The history of the lower watershed is more widely known than that of the upper watershed, but the upper watershed was actually settled soon after and became the location for most of Maxwelton's schools and gathering places.

## The First Schools

As the early settlers arrived and bore children, there came a need for schooling beyond what parents managed to do in their homes. Early records indicate that Mr. Clark, who was homesteading in the lower watershed, taught school in the late 1800s in various people's homes. The first widely recognized school in the Maxwelton area was the Island or Maxwelton School located at the corner of present day Bailey and French roads. Mary Sue Kinskie Lile knows her dad and many of the Mackie kids attended that school in the early 1900s.

J. J. Burley, Leon's father, eventually bought the old school as a home, and it stands there today next to the old Parsons place.

By 1907, the Woodland School was built farther up Maxwelton Road. When the South Whidbey School District built the Intervale School (no longer standing) in 1915 at the corner of Quade and Maxwelton roads, the Woodland School closed and became the community center–Woodland Hall.

As of this book's writing, no one is alive who attended either the Maxwelton or the Woodland School. However there are a number of living pioneers who attended the Intervale School which operated from 1915 to 1935 and was built by P. H. Mackie.

Some of those are Gerry Brixner Miller, Myron Brixner, Lincoln Wildes, Evelyn Hagstrom Varon, Janice Burley Wildes, Margaret Wildes Seals and Joe Long. Many of them still live in the watershed.

Grades one through four of the Intervale School were in one room and grades five through eight were in the other room. According to Gerry Brixner Miller it was a large, beautiful building which at its peak housed about forty children. Mrs. John Patton, Sr. taught the younger children for years. Jeanette Mackie Straub taught the older children for a while. There was a playground area and woods nearby.

*The old Maxwelton School still stands as a private residence.*

Elementary schools on the south end of the island were consolidated in 1935. All children then attended school in Langley. The Intervale School was sold to private interests and eventually destroyed. Many people in Maxwelton felt it should have been retained as a public gathering place.

No one is quite sure what year the first school bus picked up children, but in 1927, as a first-grader, Evelyn Hagstrom Varon remembers walking one mile from Swede Hill to Leon Burley's house where she and her brother Clifford boarded Burley's bus to the Intervale School. They got permission to attend Intervale rather than Glendale's Ingleside School (two and a half miles from the Hagstrom home) because the Glendale district had no bus.

Joe Long, Margaret Wildes Seals and Myron Brixner were in the first class to graduate from the newly finished Langley High School (now the middle school) in 1936. Evelyn Hagstrom Varon graduated in 1938 along with thirty other South Whidbey classmates.

## Maxwelton Churches

People in rural America found many ways to keep the tradition of worship alive even without clergy or churches. At those long family tables at the Mackie gatherings, saying grace and singing were mainstays of spiritual presence.

Seth Mackie still recollects those family gatherings. "I remember the huge, big dinners at the white house, and boy could they sing. Auntie Em especially had a spectacular voice."

John A. Brixner donated some of his land north of the Mackies to build a community gathering place that became the Free Methodist "Little Brown" Church. P. H. Mackie donated the lumber. Mackie's daughter Julia and Brixner's son Myron were the first couple married in the church in 1917.

*The "Little Brown Church" then and now.*

In Maxwelton between World War I and World War II, not everyone had cars and most folks remember walking a lot. So even though Langley had a Methodist Church by 1908 and other south end churches were springing up, people in the valley needed local places to gather for worship.

As the community grew, the American Sunday School Union helped residents establish a second place of worship at Woodland Hall. The

Sunday School Union was a national organization that sent teachers—missionaries—to rural areas to help establish places of worship.

"We averaged one hundred people at Woodland Hall some Sunday mornings," says Gerry Miller. "We sang songs, read Bible verses and shared fellowship."

Woodland Hall was closed in the 1980s. The South Whidbey School District resumed ownership and eventually sold the hall to Kim Hoelting who currently uses it to dry and store Alaskan cedar.

*Woodland Hall*

James Grubb, cousin of Floyd, has a special connection to the Little Brown Church, which was remodeled into an A-frame, then painted gray in the 1990s and renamed the Maxwelton Christian Fellowship in 2000. Grubb's Aunt Pearl and Uncle Frank DeLong, a Free Methodist minister, raised him and his sister after both their parents died.

At the time the Grubb children came to live with Pearl and Frank, Frank was preaching in Sedro Woolley. In 1940 Frank was assigned to the Little Brown Church and James remembers the shock of rural life with no electricity or bathtub. James went on to work on tugboats for 33 years, but has since retired to Maxwelton.

## The Maxwelton Stores

As settlement increased in the lower watershed, the need for a store grew stronger. Everett and Port Townsend were not convenient enough. James Edgar Montgomery arrived on Whidbey Island in 1907 and ran a general store about the time the Mackies put the dock in. It remained active for a number of years at the end of the large dock that welcomed people to Chautauqua. He also became the postmaster for the area.

*The dock, long-gone, was a focus for Maxwelton commerce.*

The Montgomerys are another family with fourth- and fifth-generation history represented on the island. James Edgar Montgomery's great-grandson Dave Montgomery, whose grand-

*Julia Brixner's early Maxwelton store.*

mother was a Mackie, still lives in the lower watershed with his wife Eileen.

The current Maxwelton store, across from Dave Mackie Park, dates back to 1931 when Julia Mackie Brixner, recovering from the death of her husband, began selling vegetables and fruits grown on her father's farm. Her father built her a small lean-to next to the cottage where she and her three children—Myron, Geraldine and Lauren—were living on the Maxwelton beach.

Being resourceful, Julia began baking breads and pies to sell. One of the first names of the little store was the "Green Gate." Shortly thereafter, Julia met and married Ray Cross. Together they expanded the store to include gas pumps. The name was changed to the "Cross Country Store" and they operated it until 1950.

Both Gerry Miller and Myron Brixner remember their mother Julia with special fondness. "She never wanted anyone to say she was a pioneer or anything," says Myron. "But she was an incredible woman. After our dad died, she had to support us three kids by creating and running the store. And before she was married, she would ride her horse Fleet up to teach school at Classic Road near Greenbank. She would teach all week and then ride home for the weekend."

*The Maxwelton store evolved over time.*

"When wealthy people from Seattle would come to the beach in the summer, they'd order chickens from the store. Mom would walk all the way up to Midvale to get one, bring it home and dress it up for them," recalls Gerry. "Sometimes she'd go down to the beach and net a salmon. She could do anything. I never had a bought dress before I was 16 and I remember her canning everything from venison to apples."

The store and cottage changed hands many times thereafter, until it was bought by Doreen and John Delano in 1987. They did extensive remodeling of the store to honor its original construction, and displayed photographs of early Maxwelton history. They operated the store for ten years, and it has changed hands several times since then.

## Food, Music and Celebrations

Born in 1921 the second child of Julia Mackie Brixner and Myron Brixner, Geraldine Brixner Miller's presence still blesses Maxwelton. Gerry speaks a lot about the freedom kids had to explore and be on their own back then. She remembers picking strawberries up on Kyllonen Hill (Campbell Road) at age nine to earn money—and not liking it—but her strongest memories are of playing on the beach.

"We played games like Run Sheep Run and Mumbly Peg and we made forts. We used kelp for our phone lines. I remember when my older brother Myron came and yanked out the kelp. I got mad and asked him what he thought he was doing, and he responded, 'You haven't paid your phone bill.'"

*Myron and Gerry*

Gerry also recalls with great fondness being part of the large Mackie clan. "We'd all gather at the big house for Thanksgiving—a table spread from the dining room into the sitting room. Grandmother Ada always cooked a big feast. I especially remember how patient grandma was and how loving all of my uncles were towards each other."

John Joseph Burley and his wife Grace Mae Storch were good friends of the Mackies. They moved with them by covered wagon from Canada to Nebraska where their oldest child, Leon, was born in 1891. From there they moved by wagon again to the Yakima Valley and on to Seattle, where the P. H. Mackies were once again their neighbors.

When P. H. and his family moved to Whidbey Island in 1905, the Burleys made regular trips to the island to visit. So it was no surprise that when Leon married Marie Phillips in 1916 they soon found their way to Whidbey to join Leon's parents, who had finally succumbed to the Mackies' prompting to join them on the island. In addition to incredible resourcefulness and hard work habits, Leon and Marie brought the special gift of music to the fledgling community.

Soon after their arrival on Whidbey Island in 1921, Marie started an orchestra. The schools didn't yet have music classes, and she wanted her children exposed to quality classical music. In her own words, "We started getting together once a week to play. We had five violins, a cello, a viola, a trombone, three trumpets, a flute, two clarinets, and a piano. I played the lead violin, and that sort of led it and kept them going. I didn't stand up. I always played."[16]

Marie managed to do this despite the demands of being a young mother and a rural housewife—cooking on a wood range and washing diapers by hand with no electricity. She canned about 500 quarts of food per year. "I had a baby then, and I'd get the other children off to school, and get the baby bathed, and then I'd practice an hour on the violin before I'd do

*Leon and Marie Burley with some of the Depression-era canning equipment from Woodland Hall.*

anything else."

Ernie Noble remembers playing saxophone for the Woodland Orchestra. "Leon and Marie were the musicians. They and a couple of others carried the rest of us," says Ernie, who managed the Langley State Bank for many years. In 2002 Ernie is a spry 93 years of age, looking forward to passing the century mark.

The music program in the Maxwelton area was given a boost when the Works Progress Administration (WPA) hired a man to start a band in Maxwelton. The Burley brothers, Robert and Richard, joined. To keep them playing after the WPA program ended, Marie took over the band as well and turned it into a marching band. Other mothers made capes for the marchers and they got some military-looking caps from the Midvale store to go along with their white pants, shirts and shoes. They even had three majorettes who marched with the band.

Leon assisted Marie by being the trumpet player in the orchestra. He also drove the school bus for three generations of South Whidbey children. He milked cows until his nineties and planted his last garden at his home at age 101.

Leon was loved and respected by everyone who knew him. "Leon was just so appreciative and curious about life. A person just enjoyed being with him," says Bill Steiner, a neighbor and longtime friend. Leon died in 1996 at age 104 at Whidbey Island Manor in Oak Harbor.

Almost everyone living in Maxwelton in the pre-World War II era remembers the community gatherings at Woodland Hall. There was no television, people had little money, and there was little mobility to do things like drive to a show. So on the weekends they gathered at Woodland Hall for music and plays. Janice Burley Wildes remembers that her mother dyed her hair for one of the monthly programs.

*Everett Green and Florence Grubb perform in "Snow White and the Seven Dwarfs" at one of the Woodland Hall birthday parties.*

Then there were the popular once-a-month birthday clubs. Myron Brixner remembers they started in 1928 and were held the third Saturday of every month. "Everyone who had a birthday since the last gathering was honored," he says. He also remembers that on the first Saturday of the month the Young People's Club was held for those age 14 and over.

Baseball games were another source of community pride. Each community—Bayview, Clinton, Langley and Maxwelton—had their own baseball team. Competition could be fierce at times. Pick-up games of baseball often happened at family gatherings. According to Darrell Green, when the Mackies had a reunion one of the main events was always a ball game between the in-laws and the "out-laws" in the family.

Community canning started at Woodland Hall during the Depression. Mrs. Langdon and Mrs. Applegate were hired by the WPA to offer assistance to local homemakers. "The reason people went there," explains Gerry Miller, "is that they had pressure canners. We all had been using boiling water baths, so this was a new thing. But, you know, I don't remember anyone ever getting botulism from home-canned stuff."

Florence Quade remembers the canning at Woodland Hall. "I did some canning up there, but I was kind of messy and the woman who ran the place was pretty fussy." She learned canning from her mother and even now her pantry is stocked with dozens and dozens of jars of canned fruit. The canning program operated for five years at Woodland Hall. In 1939 about a hundred families canned 17,093 cans of food.[17]

And, of course, the Maxwelton Fourth of July celebration has happened since 1912—every year except during World Wars I and II. "I remember that the Fourth of July was the most exciting day of the year," says Shirley Hjort Gillette, former resident of Swede Hill. "The parade back then was nothing compared to what it is now, but the food, the races, everything was so much fun."

*The Maxwelton band plays for the July 4th games.*

*Bob Blasko celebrates the role of farming in the July 4th parade.*

There are years when the Maxwelton Community Club ponders whether or not to continue the tradition, but it is still the single event which people from the rest of Whidbey Island associate with Maxwelton.

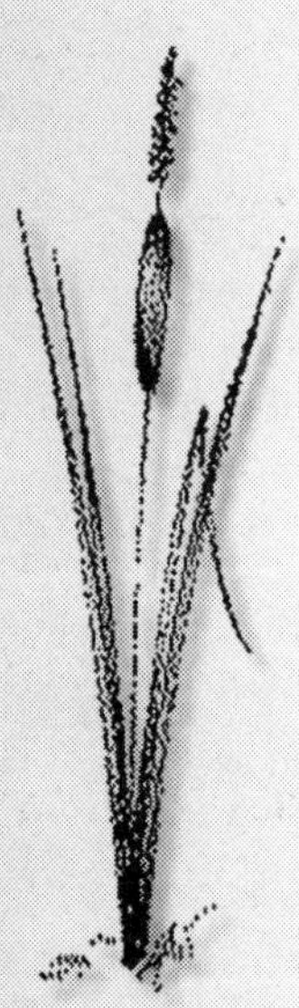

To begin again, I come back to the swamp,
To its rich decay, its calm disorder,
to alders with their reddening catkins, to hummocks
Of marsh grass floating on their own living and dead
Abundance, and wait on the shore...

Here among shotgun shells and trampled blackberries,
How can I shape, again, something from nothing?

David Wagoner, from *"Return to the Swamp"*
in *Landfall*, Atlantic-Little Brown, 1980

Maxwelton Creek and its tributaries run from above the Intermediate school, under the highway and down the length of Maxwelton Road to its outflow at the beach. It drains the high ridges from Campbell Road's Kyllonen Hill on the east to the Bayview Road/Pioneer Park ridge on the west. The creek flows year-round, as does its major tributary, Quade Creek.

A Journey Through the Maxwelton Watershed

Chapter 7

# The Upper Watershed

Early settlers to Maxwelton were drawn first to the lower watershed. It was readily accessible by the only available transportation—boats. And it contained an abundance of fresh water, wildlife, and large forests. However, it was not long before settlers created a crude system of trails and roads to the upper watershed and moved inland.

The upper watershed, generally north of Ewing Road, contains a variety of habitats—from the freshwater marshes surrounding Miller Lake to the riparian vegetation of shrubs and small trees along the creeks to the old-growth forests of the ridges.

One of the earliest and most well-known settlers of the upper watershed was Charles E. Feek. A former Seattle contractor, in 1902 he purchased from Dr. P. B. Miller 600 acres of marsh and stump land that ran from north of Miller Lake south to about Ewing Road, and included hundreds of acres of marshlands.

"This area is a sedge/peat marsh," says Ewing Road farmer Leland Long. "Miller Lake is the remnant of what was once a much larger lake. Over the years, sphagnum moss has spread out over the top of it and then sunk. My Grandfather Pontius tells stories of losing horses that would sink down into it. But gradually the marsh filled in and people were encouraged to graze cattle on it."

Feek benefited greatly from the hard work Dr. Miller had done to transform his logged-off acres into suitable farmland. At first Feek continued the truck gardening begun by Miller. One year he is said to have grown 300 large sacks of onions on one acre of land. Eventually, however, he turned to raising hay, grain and dairy cows.

Like P. H. Mackie, Feek was more than a farmer. In 1908 he and J. A. Brixner helped form the first telephone company on the island and he became its president. He was instrumental in organizing the Masonic Lodge in Langley. Feek and P. H. Mackie were both founders of the Federal Land Bank. And Feek served as South Whidbey's County Commissioner for several years.

Feek's large Victorian house—still standing on Maxwelton Road, across the street and south of Woodland Hall—was partially built by John

*Feek House seen from the marsh.*

A. Brixner in 1904. Brixner, according to his granddaughter Gerry Miller, built elegant staircases and probably did much of the fine finishing work on the mansion. Brixner came just to help on the house, but bought property nearby and stayed in Maxwelton. Feek and his family entertained many business clients in that home over the years.

## Maintaining the Creek

As was true in the lower watershed, farmers re-engineered Maxwelton Creek and all its tributaries in the upper valley. Leland Long says, "The original creek was in a gentle swale just going down the valley. To drain this, farmers made a ditch. It was prior to 1913, because it occurred about the time Grandfather Pontius came."

To the best of Leland's and his father Joe's knowledge, there never was a diking district established. The ditching was simply done by individual property owners.

They explain that once the area was farmed, the peat was destroyed by exposure to air. As it began to decay, the soil lost mass and the marsh began to settle. The bottom of the side ditches that had been dug to drain the marsh were then higher than the farm fields themselves. "We saw no sense in maintaining those laterals since they were now above the level of the fields," explains Joe. "So we took 'em out."

*In the winter of 1996, big rains caused the creek to flood, spilling out over the road near the Outdoor Classroom.*

Maxwelton Creek itself was regularly cleaned from end to end. According to Joe and Leland, Herb Gildow did most of that work with a dragline in the 1940s. Others continued the practice later.

## The "Backcountry" of the Watershed

The panic of 1893 created an economic downturn that left some people in the city wishing for land and the ability to grow enough food to feed their families. Word spread that stump land in the interior of South Whidbey with a number of abandoned loggers' cabins could be had for next to nothing. And so, the settlers came into the back lands behind Glendale, Cultus Bay and Maxwelton.

While there were some wealthy families, most of the people who came to the Maxwelton watershed then had little more than hope for a better life and an incredible willingness to work hard. And one of the things that makes Maxwelton a viable community into the twenty-first century is that a number of the families who settled in the area remained for generations.

### Kyllonen Hill

In 1889 Herman Kyllonen homesteaded 160 acres atop the 300-foot hill that divides two watersheds. Having left Finland less than a decade earlier, he made his living by logging cordwood for the steamers coming in and out of Langley. In 1892 he married another native Finlander, Finna. Together they built a large house and sauna that provided a community gathering place for potlucks and dancing.

After harvesting the trees from his land, he sold it in 40-acre tracts and turned his own thirty acres into a productive farm. The Kyllonens had three

*A Finnish farmhouse is at the center of the Chinook land.*

children and were known for their community spirit and fierce integrity. When they received the bid to clear the land for the Woodland School in 1907, they kept to their bid of $400 even though the dynamite for blasting the stumps cost more than the bid itself. In addition, they donated four acres of their property for the schoolyard.

Part of the Kyllonen land is protected today as a teaching and learning center. In 1966 Fritz and Vivienne Hull purchased 15 acres of the Pietila family land atop Kyllonen Hill, including the original farm buildings and sauna, and founded the Chinook Learning Center.

Now renamed the Whidbey Institute, this non-profit center is a kind of modern-day version of Chautauqua, sponsoring many educational and spiritual events. Over the years it has grown to about 100 acres with many hiking trails and an expanded community hall for larger lectures.

Settlers on and near Kyllonen Hill included Virgil and Mabel Auvil, Charles Fleming, John Minner, B. D. and Grace Prentice, and Floyd and Mary Galbreath. The Auvils dammed what is now known as Quade Creek, creating a series of small lakes for fish hatcheries, and later raised both baby chicks and mink.

Florence Quade remembers walking up the road in her younger years to swim with her two young girls near the Auvils' ponds. Charles Fleming raised strawberries. John Minner raised goats. The Prentices started a fish hatchery and a farm and later brought in their daughter and son-in-law, the Galbreaths, to help.

**Ewing Road**

In 1908 Sidney and Jack Nourse purchased 40 acres of land from Roy Newell at the corner of Ewing and Maxwelton roads. In the next few years brothers Tom, Alfred and Harry joined them as they created the "Nourse Brothers Ranch." Their parents, Thomas and Elizabeth, sailed from England to join their sons.

The Nourses were active in their new community. Older brother Tom wrote and directed several plays presented at Woodland Hall, in addition to establishing a thriving flower bulb business. Sidney built the Midvale store and served as a notary public and justice of the peace.

Tom and his wife Mae had three daughters and one son, Pat. After his service in World War II, Pat lived on the family farm and commuted to his job at the Oak Harbor Naval Base. Pat married Lucille Thompson, from a pioneer Bayview family. Pat and Lucille managed the family farm until Pat retired in 1978. Lucille still lives in the Maxwelton watershed and was honored in the Island County Fair Distinguished Senior Citizens program in 2002.

*Lucille Nourse*

## Chicken & Egg Farms

Though the Feeks and the Mackies held large tracts of land, they were so involved in other pursuits that farming remained a secondary concern for them. Most of the people who settled in early Maxwelton had smaller acreage and farmed as a means to feed their families.

"Everyone had a garden. You had to, to live," says Florence Quade. Florence and Edgar Quade were the first settlers on what is now Quade Road, and kept themselves busy with 44 fruit trees, a couple of cows, goats, and one little sheep.

But there were at least two Maxwelton families who tackled farming as large, full-time operations—the Pattons in the lower watershed and the Longs in the upper watershed.

### The Pattons

John Patton, Sr. bought his land in 1909. His wife, Martha, taught the lower grades at the Intervale School. For a time they ran a small store on the corner of their property at Sills and Maxwelton roads. They carried everything from candy to livestock feed. In 1926 when their son John Jr. was twelve they bought 200 Rhode Island Reds. Slowly they expanded the operation until they had over 100,000 chickens.

Dorothy Patton, wife of John Jr., reminisces about the many decades they spent being full-time chicken farmers. "I was a city girl and it took a little getting used to," she said. John Jr. fell in love with her when she came to the island as a summer teacher for the American Sunday School Union and he was the Sunday School superintendent at Woodland Hall. They were married in 1946. "Actually at one time I said, 'Either the chickens go or I go.' I notice that we all stayed."

"By the late 1950s or early '60s you had to go big or get out of the chicken business," continues Dorothy. "It was hard work and there were precious few vacations. We hired local kids to do everything from washing eggs to spreading feed, but the bottom line was we had to oversee things." Dorothy retired before John. "He told me he'd retire when he no longer enjoyed what he was doing." John died of cancer in 1994 at the age of 80.

*The gravestone of John Patton, Jr. in the Bayview Cemetery reflects his long association with chickens.*

John Patton, Jr. was highly thought of by valley residents. Roy Hagglund, lifelong Maxwelton resident now living in Midvale, says, "I don't know if there ever was a better man than John Patton. People wanted to model themselves after him. He never said a bad word about anybody. He was a prince of a guy, one of a kind."

### The Longs

One large farm still in existence at the turn of the twenty-first century is the Longs' 200 acres along Ewing Road on the west side of Maxwelton Creek. Joe Long moved to part of that piece of land in August 1926 with his recently widowed mother Nancy and two brothers.

His mother had arrived to be a housekeeper for bachelor Claus Brower who was managing the Feek farm at the time. Eventually Claus and Joe's mother were married. Joe and his older brother were enrolled at the Intervale School.

Joe got into the chicken business at an early age. His mother got some cull chickens from Percy

Wilkinson and fed them cottage cheese, oatmeal and such. They prospered and she gave them to her boys to learn to care for them.

When her neighbors and friends, the Pontius family, decided to move in 1930 Nancy said her boys would like to buy the land. "We picked strawberries for 1/4 cent per pound to save money," says Joe. Back then all the stump farms had a half dozen cows, 500 chickens and strawberries.

The Pontius family was to figure in Joe Long's life in significant ways. Their daughter Leda, who had left home to get a teaching certificate, and Joe were married in 1947. So Leda returned to her Maxwelton childhood home with Joe and they set up a chicken business. They had two children and, by 1976, about 130,000 chickens.

*The Long-Pontius family, Joe Long far right, Leland Long far left, and their chickens.*

As Joe's son Leland explains, "We had to make the decision several times to either get bigger or get out. We marketed routinely about 40,000 dozen eggs per week for decades. Eventually we were so automated that the first person to touch an egg was the housewife as she took her egg from the carton in the store."

In 1989 they began to phase out by not adding any more stock. According to Joe and Leland, part of their problem was being too small and too out of position. The Midwest had long been considered the egg basket of the nation because it had the land to raise cheap and abundant grain. However in the early years the Midwest, because of the weather, could produce eggs only in the spring and the summer. The rest of the year eggs were preserved in cold storage and shipped by railroad to the coasts.

That worked fine until the Depression came and people on the coasts found that they could keep a few chickens, feed them grain and have fresh eggs year-round. Coastal chicken farmers picked up on the idea of "farm fresh" and all of a sudden they were in business.

The advantage to the Long and Patton farms was short-lived, though. In the 1970s, 18-wheeler trucks started shipping eggs from the Midwest to the coasts on the recently completed interstate highways. "Once they could put fresh eggs in the stores in 36 hours at 7 to 8 cents a dozen less than us, it spelled a death knell for most poultry farms out here," concludes Leland. "The fun was gone from farming."

Today Joe at 81 is the only one farming full-time. He plants the corn and tends to the small herd of cattle they run. Leland and his son, who live in houses adjoining Joe and Leda's, work together driving trucks and help out Joe after hours.

With the changes in these two farming families, Maxwelton is once again an area of small farms with people managing livestock and crops mostly part-time.

And we go out as the fish go out, leaving the taste
of the rivers we know, joining the dark invisible weight
of what we would become, the calm sense of movement
seeing the others forming our shoals, and the scales
on our sides filling the depths with trembling stars.

In that depth, return's instinctual, the moon harvests
the long years and binds them into sheaves in a circle,
and we return too, for home from the sea we come to the river,
turning the ocean's face toward the land, opening to silence
as the salmon opens to the sweet water in a saltless stream.

David Whyte,
from "Time Left Alone"
In *Where Many Rivers Meet*
Many Rivers Press, 1999

*Fish traps such as this were made by the San Juan Fishing & Packing Company on the Maxwelton dock for years.*

A Journey Through the Maxwelton Watershed

Chapter 8

# The Bounty of the Watershed

When European-Americans arrived in the Maxwelton watershed in the 1870s, they found an ecosystem little changed by the light use of native peoples. They replaced the hunter/gatherer economy of the Snohomish with an economy based on logging and farming. This new economy would greatly impact the traditional endeavors of fishing and hunting, but it did not eliminate them altogether, for fishing and hunting have always been part of the rural ethic of America.

In Jacob Anthes' description of tending the Quinn homestead in 1880 he describes the bounty of the watershed: "Game such as deer, pheasants, ducks and geese was plentiful, and I could spear a salmon in the slough with a sharp stick. So I lived on fresh meat and fish almost entirely."

A century later there would still be a deer-hunting season in Maxwelton, but there would be no spearing of salmon in the slough. One hundred years of logging, farming and settlement would change the ecosystem to the advantage of some wildlife and to the disadvantage of others.

## The Salmon Remember

*All successful salmon develop highly specific adaptation to the rivers they frequent. They know through the genetic legacy of their parents where to hide, what their prey looks like, when to run to the sea and when to return. Since every river is unique in its flow pattern and terrain, every run of wild salmon is necessarily different genetically from all others.*[18]

No creature knows the subtleties of the Maxwelton watershed like its wild salmon. They know where the gentle sloping gravel with cool water lies to lay their eggs. These stretches of gravel hide the tiny "alevins" that emerge from the eggs still attached to their yolk sacs. After a couple of weeks, the yolk sac is absorbed. The inch-long young "fry" then enter the larger, precarious world of Maxwelton Creek. Reacting instinctively out of their genetic memory, the fry know how to dodge larger fish, water birds and snakes.

Two species of salmon have linked their genetic instincts and life cycles to the Maxwelton watershed: coho (or silver) and chum. One type of Pacific trout is found in the watershed: the

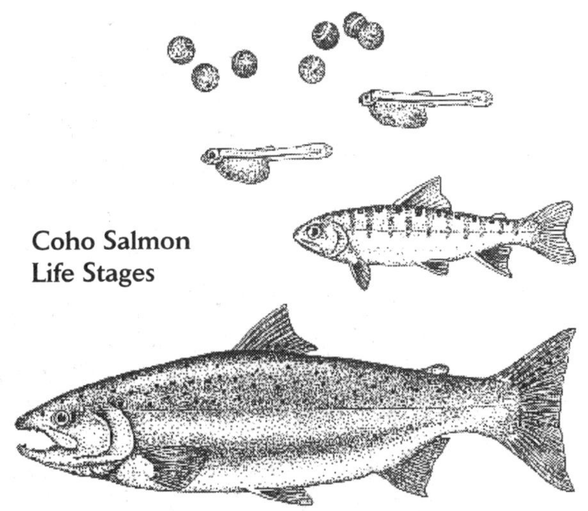

Coho Salmon
Life Stages

sea-run cutthroat. All three are anadromous—that is, living their lives in both salt and fresh water.

The coho fry hatch in the upper watershed and remain there up to two years before migrating to salt water. The chum fry almost immediately make their way down to the lower watershed. When it is time to make the transition from fresh water to salt water—a biological transition that few creatures can manage—the fry are called smolt.

The sea-run cutthroat trout behave differently. They go back and forth between fresh and salt water, spawning in the fresh water and then returning to the salt water to feed. Sea-run cutthroats have the advantage of a large prey base at sea, so they can become much larger than landlocked cutthroat.

*Cutthroat trout*

Jan Holbrook, a biologist who does fish counts for the Maxwelton Salmon Adventure, caught a 16-inch cutthroat in 1999 that was clearly returning to the sea. "Once outside, the cutthroat use the nearshore marine environment of the eel grass and prey on forage fish like herring, sand lance and smelt," she says.

The life of a smolt is completely different from one watershed of salmon to the next. On a river like the Yukon in Alaska, schools of smolt travel at night until they find the sea—a distance of 1,800 miles. In a watershed like Maxwelton, they may swim only ten to twelve miles.

A smolt's life is precarious at best. Survival rates in the healthiest of watersheds are rarely greater than one in a hundred. Smolts can be killed by predators and by nitrogen-rich or warm, oxygen-depleted water. To mature into adults, smolts must make their way to the mouth of the stream or river which has nurtured them.

**Salmon Life Cycle**

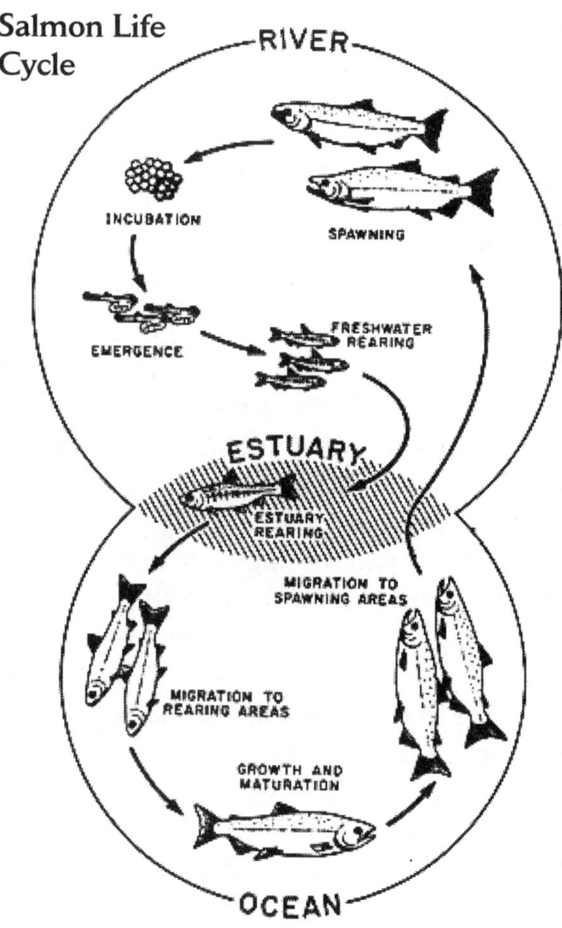


Before the dike was built in 1914 and a tidegate installed at the mouth of Maxwelton Creek, chum, coho and sea-run cutthroats had a 200-acre estuary with regular flushes of salt water in which to make the transition from fresh water to seawater. Since that time, their estuary has decreased to the point where they have almost no transition zone to prepare them for life at sea.

Once smolts reach an estuary and their bodies begin to experience the salt water mixing with fresh water, complex physiological changes must take place. In the estuary their diet also changes, as they feed on minute zooplankton and gradually larger creatures like crustaceans and shrimp. A healthy estuary is absolutely essential in the life cycle of the salmon.

But it is not only chum, coho and sea-run cutthroat that use the Maxwelton watershed. Recent science suggests that the nearshore marine environment, just beyond the Maxwelton beach, is an important nursery for young salmon of several species.

Pink, chum, and Chinook salmon that enter marine waters as juveniles, or fry that hatch in rivers like the Skagit and the Snohomish, spend considerable time growing and feeding in the waters off Whidbey Island.

So there was and is a kind of salmon nursery happening offshore that is very important to the health of salmon in the entire region. In pre-tidegate days, it is likely that these young salmon from other rivers moved in and out of the estuary to feed and grow on their way to open waters.

## Salmon in the Creek

There are several historic references to salmon in Maxwelton Creek, in addition to Anthes' letter. In oral histories collected by the Maxwelton Salmon Adventure in the late 1980s and early 1990s, Pat Nourse talked about watching his folks pitchfork dead salmon from the creek bed onto the garden for fertilizer. Another long-time watershed resident, Esther Erikson, described seeing live salmon in the creek.

"Rand and I bought our place across from the creek in '37. There were fish—the kids used to fish. I remember the year the fish came up so fast that you could almost walk across on them up to the lake. And there was no culvert to bother them. They went right through up to the lake," she explained. "We could hear them coming, splashing up the creek. It was just full of fish."

Pat Nourse's folks were probably using spawned-out adults of chum salmon for fertilizer. (Chum are nicknamed "dog salmon" because most people believe their inferior taste and texture warrants feeding them only to dogs.)

Esther Erikson was probably seeing and hearing spawning cohos if they indeed were heading up to Miller Lake. Jacob Anthes' 1880 description of "water alive with salmon as far as the eye could reach" was near the saltwater estuary and could have been describing a fall run of either chum or coho.

Albert "Abe" Luhn, third owner of property settled in 1889 in the middle of the watershed, remembers that the people from whom he bought the property were poor and subsisted on salmon from the creek. The old smokehouse still stands on his property.

"Resilient" is the one word that best describes salmon. They have survived ten million years[19] of volcanic eruptions, earthquakes, glacial advances, geomagnetic reversals and the arrival of Euro-Americans. It is only the latter event that has brought some salmon species to the brink of extinction.

In the pre-European landscape of the Pacific Northwest, salmon were central to the food chain of several species: orcas, seals, bear, eagles, and humans. People began to notice and harvest salmon soon after the Vashon Glacier retreated.

The Snohomish tribe of the Salish at Cultus Bay fished for salmon as far away as the Straits of Juan de Fuca and as close as the Snohomish River and Maxwelton Creek. Over time the Snohomish improved their methods of fishing by using nets and wiers. Learning to smoke the meat to preserve it as a year-round staple for their diet was a huge advancement.

*Salmon hangs on racks at this native fishing village.*

## Fish Traps

Native peoples fished with great respect for the salmon, which served as the essential meat that defined their culture. They had devised careful rituals of catching, eating, preserving and ceremonially burying the fish to ensure their annual return. To them the reappearance of the salmon was a miracle they did not take for granted. Their population numbers were small and sustainable and they took only enough fish to feed themselves.

The Snohomish from the Digwadsh village at Cultus Bay either scooped up baskets of the fish as they made their way up the narrow mouth of Maxwelton Creek or they speared them. On larger rivers native peoples built weirs—simple handmade fences—to catch the migrating salmon.

The history of European-American commercial fishing is a story of competition: the determination to be the first to access fish populations and to take as much of the "crop" as current technology would allow them to get to the market.[20]

Just as Euro-Americans believed there was no end to the immense forests of the Pacific Northwest, so they also believed there would never be an end to the massive salmon runs. Their methods of catching salmon reflected this attitude.

Fish traps were the first technology developed to capture the great salmon migration. They were placed in front of the native people's weirs—just beyond the mouths of rivers and creeks.

Fish traps joined logging as one of the first industries in the Maxwelton watershed. The San Juan Fishing and Packing Company had a small fish trap construction operation on the beach at Maxwelton in the early 1900s. Completed fish traps were sold and distributed all over Puget Sound.

Fish were literally herded into these traps by the thousands. According to Myron Brixner, his mother Julia recalled traps in the pre-World War I days that could catch up to 35,000 salmon at a time. "Mother said sometimes they had to open the traps and let the fish go so the sheer weight of the fish would not break the traps."

Darrell Green recalls that there were several cabins on the long sand spit that paralleled the early creek mouth. He described them as cabins used by the fishermen who tended the fish traps.

Fish traps were still in operation in the early 1930s when Julia Mackie Brixner opened the Green Gate Store. People would call her on the phone to order salmon. She would paddle out to one of the fish traps and place an order with the watchman tending the trap.

"She sold salmon to people for 75 cents for a whole king, 35 cents for a coho, 25 cents for a chum and 10 cents for pinks or humpies," explains her son, Myron. "Fish were cheap because they were so abundant. Many people then canned the fish at the WPA cannery at Woodland Hall."

In 1934, fish traps were made illegal in Puget Sound. By that time gill-netters, one-man operations in small boats, were catching fish out be-

*Julia Mackie Brixner Cross*

yond the fish traps. Purse seiners, with bigger boats and a crew, fished at different times from the gill-netters. Finally, the trollers with big bottom-fishing dragnets pursued schools of salmon into the ocean itself.

As early as 1875, it was well-known that the complete collapse of the Atlantic salmon fisheries was due to failure to regulate fishing and protect habitat. Yet for the next century the Pacific Northwest would follow the same course of overfishing and failure to protect habitat.

## Dogfish Livers

In the early 1940s, with World War II raging and many men serving abroad, income was nearly as hard to come by in Maxwelton as it had been during the Depression. A brief bonanza occurred in 1942-43 when people discovered that the oil from livers of dogfish (a small form of shark) could be sold at a good price. The dogfish were abundant and easy to catch, so many people got in on the act.

"There was a run of dogfish in the early '40s," explains Lincoln Wildes. "People seined for them off the beach." He remembers that people got 13 cents a pound for the livers reportedly used for "cod"-liver oil. The bonanza was short-lived because an artificial means of producing cod-liver oil was invented.

Leon Burley spoke at length about the dogfish in *The Formative Years* by Nancy Donnelly.[21] "The best time for fishing was when the tide was going out. You could hear them in the night, clicking like they do, a sound they make with their mouths. Dogfish would get together and drive schools of herring toward the beach, where they couldn't dive and get away. We'd get in the shallows out behind the dogfish, and while they fed on herring we'd spear them with gaffs, pitchforks, whatever."

Leon described how one night by moonlight he put out his net and caught so many he couldn't lift the net. He had to come back the next morning with a winch to get them to shore before the tide came in again. He said he earned about $200 for the livers, plus some money for the carcasses.

Minus their livers, the dogfish were taken to the Sea Products Company fertilizer plant (the "stink plant") at Cultus Bay for processing. The plant processed the dogfish and spoiled salmon from Seattle canneries to extract oil that was used in paints and other manufactured goods. At its peak the plant employed fifteen people. In the mid-1950s it closed and the machinery was barged to Alaska.

## Shellfish Harvests

"'The tide's out, the table is set' was my parents' saying," said Pat Nourse in an interview conducted by the Maxwelton Salmon Adventure. From the earliest days, settlers relied on the abundance of the sea much as their native predecessors had. Descendants of early settlers who live in Maxwelton today still talk about their parents harvesting clams, oysters and crabs as a regular part of "living off the land."

"I remember my mother and grandmother harvesting clams and canning clam chowder," recalls Diane McDonald Tinker. She admits, "I don't like clams to this day."

Lincoln and Janice Burley Wildes remember Herb Green selling crabs for a time, but generally agreed that nobody in Maxwelton really made a living fishing or crabbing.

*Brothers Ivan and Lyle Mackie ready for a hunt.*

A Journey Through the Maxwelton Watershed

Chapter 9

# An Abundant Wildlife Corridor

The Maxwelton watershed is a rural wildlife corridor.[22] Healthy populations of deer, raccoons, hawks, owls, ducks and most songbirds abound. Hunting seasons on deer, pheasant and ducks still exist.

In large part, the health of wildlife populations is due to the presence of agricultural lands, private woodlots and open spaces such as large gardens. On a summer day, it is not uncommon to hear the kew-kew-kew of a soaring redtail hawk. At dusk little brown bats begin their nightly forays for flying insects.

While some species are doing well, others are challenged by the encroachment of civilization. Still other species have vanished from the watershed.

## Columbian black-tailed deer

This most common deer subspecies in the Pacific Northwest is easily observed on all of Whidbey Island. They prefer brushy, logged lands and coniferous forests. Columbian black-tailed deer have been here since the landscape belonged to the native peoples, and they have managed to co-exist with today's more heavily landscaped settlement.

Early Maxwelton settlers relied on venison to supplement their diet. Jacob Anthes described killing a deer in 1880. "I remember hunting a lot with my dad [Clayton Howard Mackie]," says Seth Mackie. "He got a bolt-action rifle for $10 from Sears and Roebuck and he took venison when he needed it."

Myron Brixner shares that while he was growing up he "ate a lot of deer meat honestly and dishonestly." He remembers taking venison

*Black-tailed deer by Finnish sauna on Chinook land.*

sandwiches to grade school. Abe Luhn's family leased Feek's acres in the lower watershed for hunting for many years. Hunting for deer in the Maxwelton watershed occurs today, but the season is short and the lands open to hunting are limited.

Today deer are about the biggest form of wildlife that people encounter. Their aesthetic beauty is appreciated and admired, although their fondness for garden and landscape plants tries some people's patience.

### Coyotes

Trapper Fred Goodman caught his first coyote on Whidbey Island in the 1970s. Joe Long believes coyotes were introduced on the north end of Whidbey Island and made their way down to Maxwelton by the late 1970s.

Roy Hagglund of Midvale observes that coyotes are present in the valley in great numbers now, though he never saw them in earlier times. Others feel strongly that coyotes made their way across the Deception Pass bridge. Yet another theory is that they swam across Dugwalla Bay at a minus tide. The truth may be some combination of the three.

In the Pacific Northwest, these intelligent and adaptable animals manage to occupy almost every habitat type, from open ranch country to dense forests to downtown waterfronts. Despite ever-increasing human encroachment and past efforts to eliminate coyotes, the species maintains its numbers and is increasing in some areas.

Contrary to popular belief, coyotes are usually solitary. The so-called "bands" or "packs" of coyotes are almost always family groups composed of a mother and her young. During the mating period in late winter a group may also be composed of a female and several males.

Coyotes are opportunists, both as night hunters and as scavengers. They eat any small animal they can capture. Grass, fruits, and berries are eaten during summer and fall. They are known to eat pet food, garbage, garden crops, poultry, and pets (mostly cats). For this reason, coyotes are a controversial subject on South Whidbey.

### The Vanished

Although it is officially the state mammal of Washington, *elk* were gone from the Maxwelton watershed by the time the first settlers arrived in 1870. "The decline of elk had begun with the introduction of the gun among the Salish, but white hunters completed the destruction of the animal in the 1850s."[23]

Quite possibly the number of elk on the island was small to begin with. As the second largest land mammals found in the Pacific Northwest (only moose are larger), elk require large amounts of food because of their body size and herding tendencies. Even though the island contained elk habitat—grasslands and clear-cuts interspersed with closed canopy forests—it was still a small, confined area for such large animals.

The *wolf* was also gone from Maxwelton by the time the first settlers arrived. Describing the settlers' hatred of wolves as "automatic, almost instinctive," historian Richard White attributes the extermination of wolves to the $3 bounty Island County government set on them in 1855. "The wolves that howled near W. S. Ebey's cabin in 1856 had, by the end of the decade, been destroyed or driven from the county."

The other mammal that could not co-exist with human settlement on the island was the *black bear*. Bears lasted longer than either elk or wolves, but the last validated sightings of them are from the 1940s. Lincoln Wildes remembers seeing a mother and two cubs on Wildes Road when he was six years old (1932). Esther Erikson described having a bearskin from an animal that her father-in-law shot over at Deer Lake. And Roy Hagglund saw a bear down in Clinton when he was "real little"—the early '40s.

It isn't hard to imagine that increasing population pressure in Maxwelton increased bear/human interactions. Though bears' diets consist mostly of vegetation, they are omnivores and eat both plants and animals. Unlike the carnivorous wolf, though, they typically do not prey on sheep or cattle so they did not achieve bounty status. Eventually, decreasing habitat and hunting pressure caused the demise of the black bear in the Maxwelton watershed.

In the early and mid-1900s, *eastern red foxes* were introduced throughout the Pacific Northwest by hunting clubs and farmers who raised them for their valuable pelts. Released foxes and escapees established populations from Oregon and Washington to British Columbia, including the Maxwelton valley.

Fred Goodman, a trapper who has lived on Whidbey Island his entire life, started fox trapping when he was 10 years old (1965). The last year he caught a fox was in the mid- to late-1980s.

These dates agree with observations made by a number of local residents. Joe Long saw his first red fox in 1958 on his land. Lincoln Wildes remembers seeing fox in the 1950s. He believes they were introduced by folks in Coupeville seeking to control the population of eastern cottontail rabbit which was introduced to western Washington as a game animal beginning in the 1930s.

Both Long and Wildes thought it had been fifteen or twenty years since they had seen a red fox in the valley. The foxes' residency in Maxwelton was relatively short-lived. Once coyotes were introduced, they could not compete for food. However, cottontail rabbits continue to flourish.

## The Missing Birds

Janice Burley Wildes remembers serving pheasant to company for dinner. "Lincoln would shoot a couple of birds and if it didn't look like enough, well, it was easy to go get another." More recently, though, pheasants have been scarce in Maxwelton. There are many reasons for this—coyote predation, the reduced emphasis on pen-rearing and release of birds, human encroachment on pheasant habitats, and clean farming practices that eliminated food sources.

Jacob Anthes' letter describes seeing pheasants in the lower watershed marsh of 1880. Ring-necked pheasants, native to Asia, were not introduced in this country until 1882, so it is unlikely that Anthes actually saw pheasants. He wrote his long letter to Coupeville historian George

Kellogg nearly three decades after the event. In those thirty years, pheasants were introduced to the island so it is not so surprising that he might think pheasants were actually on the island when he first came.

Interviews of longtime valley residents revealed that many of them clearly remember hearing a lot of meadowlarks when they were growing up. Without any prompt other than "Are there any species of animal that you miss from your growing-up years?" a number of them specifically mentioned meadowlarks.

Myron Brixner said, "The thing I miss most is that wonderful song of the meadowlark. I also miss the bluebirds."

"As a kid, I remember seeing meadowlarks and bluebirds," responded Joe Long. "All of those are gone now."

"The meadowlarks sang very loud when I was a kid," responded Roy Hagglund. Lincoln and Janice Wildes also remembered hearing meadowlarks as children.

It is said that the song of a meadowlark is so clear that it can be heard through an open car window traveling at 60 miles per hour. As one of the most distinctive of bird songs, many people can identify it. But where have the meadowlarks gone?

Steve Ellis, Whidbey Audubon member and local birding expert, is intrigued with the observation about the loss of meadowlarks in the Maxwelton area. He says that meadowlarks are generally declining along with all grassland species.

"The two major causes for that are the introduction of large farming equipment and the decline of habitat," says Steve. "Meadowlarks nest on the ground in fields or under bushes. They are very vulnerable to any change in farming be it bigger equipment or changing harvest times." Increasing population generally means more cats, which are especially tough on ground-nesting birds.

Ellis says that meadowlarks are still occasionally seen near Crockett Lake and Crescent Harbor, but as far as he knows they no longer nest anywhere on Whidbey Island.

*Leaving Seattle for Whidbey Island with the Smith Tower in the background.*

A Journey Through the Maxwelton Watershed

Chapter 10

# In the Shadow of Seattle

Change can happen suddenly—or subtly. Overnight a beaver dam is built and a farmer's field is submerged under four inches of water. Or, one day a person notices that meadowlarks haven't been singing in his field for years.

Whether it happens quickly or slowly, change is the norm in life. Whether a change is for better or for worse often depends on one's point of view. But none of us seem to come by change easily.

In the last half of the twentieth century many changes came to the Maxwelton watershed. The 1950s were a pivotal time. There were still good-sized gatherings of folks at Woodland Hall for community social events. There were still children running barefoot most of the summer on Maxwelton Beach—unconcerned about yards or fences because few people lived there. And roads in the valley were still poor enough that people didn't travel all that much.

By the turn into the twenty-first century, all of these attributes of island life have changed. Woodland Hall is now privately owned. Beach lots have become highly prized and expensive. People think nothing of traveling to Seattle and back in a day. And people no longer know all their neighbors.

Clinton Ferry Dock, circa 1935

## Outside Changes

Most of the events that caused so much change in Maxwelton were not local in nature. One of the biggest was the availability of faster transportation. Airplanes, state ferry service and freeways combined to remove the buffer of isolation around Maxwelton.

The first automobiles came to Maxwelton after 1915. The arrival of the auto brought the need for better roads, and brought pressure on the available boat service to the island. The first passenger car ferries began arriving about 1919.

By 1951 the ferry system was run by the state, and in the last two decades service has increased to nearly round-the-clock, seven days a week. The Deception Pass Bridge, built in 1936, added to the island's connection to the mainland.

The completion of Interstate 5 in 1962, just in time for the World's Fair in Seattle, was another milestone of change for Maxwelton. As Joe and Leland Long explained earlier, the interstate system and fast-moving semi-trailer trucks spelled the demise of the chicken egg businesses in Maxwelton. Better roads and ferry service also meant people could begin to hold jobs off the island.

The Boeing Plant in Everett, built in 1966, created a number of off-island jobs within reasonable commuting distance. "As more jobs became available off-island, people started to get rid of their cows," says Roy Hagglund. "When they worked out, they could afford to buy milk and butter and other things."

From 1964 to 1969 the number of farms in Island County dwindled from 441 to 240 with only 80 considered productive.[24] The subsistence way of living began giving way to a more urban lifestyle as many people switched from being on the island full-time to commuting off-island.

Another change in Maxwelton's relationship to the outside world came through communication. In the early 1900s people's basic connection to the mainland and general American culture came through the radio. "As a little kid [born in 1938] I remember my folks listening to Fibber McGee and Molly on the radio," says Roy Hagglund. "We didn't dare talk until the program was over."

"We were lucky to have a radio as kids," echoes Gerry Brixner Miller. "My brother loved to listen to the baseball games."

The arrival of television in Maxwelton homes in the mid to late 1950s brought entertainment and news of the outside world at an unprecedented level. No longer isolated from the world, Maxwelton residents didn't have the same need for the Maxwelton Orchestra, the Woodland Hall birthday parties and plays, or the American Sunday School gatherings. The pioneering era of self-sufficiency and tightly-knit community was fading.

The first telephone office on South Whidbey opened in Langley in 1906. The first phones were all on a party line. Early residents recollect picking up the phone and hearing a dozen clicks. "People would drop what they were doing and listen in on the party line," said Shirley Hjort Gillette.

In 1953 David Henny III bought the phone company from Ernie and Ralph Noble and put all the lines underground. This not only greatly improved phone service, but it paved the way for computer lines into nearly every home—another level of communication with the outside world that eventually brought the opportunity for some to become full-time islanders again—as telecommuters.

The greatest outside change might arguably be the huge regional population growth. In 1950 Seattle had about 500,000 people and the population of surrounding communities was 100,000. By 1996 the ratio had reversed itself. The outlying areas had grown to 2.9 million people while the population of the city remained the same.[25] This phenomenal growth has affected nearly all aspects of Maxwelton's rural life. Local residents live in the shadow of the impact, demand—and opportunity—created by that large a neighbor.

## Changing Farm Life

Joe Long has described in detail the transition from full-time to part-time farming. Actually, though, eighty-one-year-old Joe still works full-time on his farm.

Riding along Ewing Road on a warm August day, one can easily see the fruits of his labor. A field of corn stands seven feet tall. The late afternoon shadows of surrounding trees cast a lengthening hue on his field of alfalfa. A herd of Black Angus cattle graze lazily on the edge of Maxwelton Creek. And the three generations of Long family homes stand side by side watching over this land. The beauty and continuity of their work is a treasure in the valley.

Two generations of Long family homes.

Right, Maxwelton Farm.

Some part-time farmers here have found creative ways to continue farming the land they love so deeply.

### Bill Steiner

Hal Steiner purchased 177 acres in the lower watershed from Clayton Howard Mackie in the early 1950s. Clayton Howard had inherited the family farm but he couldn't pay the taxes on the land and was heading to British Columbia to pursue his logging career. So he approached Hal, whom he knew because the Steiners owned a cabin on the Maxwelton beach. Hal went to his good friend Eddie Teale, founder of the Vitamilk company, and together they purchased the property.

Hal Steiner and Eddie Teale hired Ted Rice to manage the place, as they both lived on the mainland. The old Mackie farmhouse on the corner of Swede Hill and Maxwelton roads was remodeled, the bottomlands were plowed up and the ditches were cleaned out. Hal's sons worked on the land during the summer and on weekends. They literally brought the farm back to life and began putting up hay and raising Holstein heifers.

The farm especially flourished under the guidance of its next caretaker, Grant Borden. For thirty years Grant worked to establish a herd of 150 dairy cattle. In the late 1980s, the U.S. government offered a buy-out program because there was a surplus of milk on the market. Grant sold his herd and the farm went into its next stage of transition.

At the time of Grant's departure, the Steiners and the Teales divided their land. The Steiners took the 37 acres of marsh and upland and the Teales took the barn and the lowland. Hal's son Bill, who had taken the greatest interest in the farm, took over its management.

Bill loved being in Maxwelton. He remembers working as a child for fifty cents to clean up sawdust at the Evergreen Mill and then going to spend his hard-earned money at the Cross Country Store. And of course he remembers helping out on the family farm every time his family came out to the island.

*Bill Steiner on Leon Burley's hayrake.*

One of the things he loved best was working with Leon Burley. "Leon was so accepting of ideas and possibilities. He recited poetry by rote and he had this amazing whistle you could hear for miles," says Bill. "I know Marie fed me more times than she should have."

Bill taught history for the Edmonds School District, and his wife Nancy worked on Mercer Island. They moved to the valley with their sons Matt and John, and eventually Bill got a job with the South Whidbey School District. Bill now raises his own hay and registered Polled Herefords. In the valley's fine tradition of creative small farming, he has recently begun growing trees for nurseries.

**Claudia Vander Pol**

When Ed Teale and Hal Steiner split their land, Teale's oldest son was busy as president of Vitamilk Dairy and his youngest son was a musician. So his daughter, Claudia Vander Pol, took over managing the farm.

"Grant stayed on a couple of years after selling his dairy herd and actually built up a small herd of beef cattle," explains Claudia with great respect for Grant's skill and knowledge. "He moved on and left us our percentage of cows, but we only fed them local hay and they didn't thrive."

Like Bill, Claudia has fond memories of her childhood summers in the valley. Her love in life as a young girl was horses. Her father's purchase of the land enabled her lifelong dream of owning a horse to come true. "I spent my junior high years on Prince," she said. "I didn't even know I was in Maxwelton. I was simply on Prince."

One of the people Claudia remembers most fondly was Florence Langworthy, daughter of P. H. and Ada Mackie. "Florence called us the 'foreigners' because we lived in Seattle. She lived in that house on the corner of Maxwelton and

Swede Hill and had a garden in the sand. She never wasted anything—she watered her garden with water from the wash and she sent old squares of bright clothing off to Africa. Her whole house always smelled like the soap she was making. She was a real special lady."

Claudia hired Don Curtis, who had worked for Grant, to run the farm. Meanwhile, she studied the cattle market and attended seminars. "The one thing I could see was that there was always a steady price for dairy heifers," she says. "I also studied intensive grazing management—dividing your land into smaller sections, letting the cows eat the grass down to the proper height and then moving them on to the next section."

With the help of Don and her son Justin, they divided their 65 acres into three-acre parcels and began grazing the heifers. "All the old-time farmers told me that wasn't the way to do it," explains Claudia. "First, I had to battle being a woman. Second, I was doing things in a way that was not real popular and I had to convince the men working for me to do it that way."

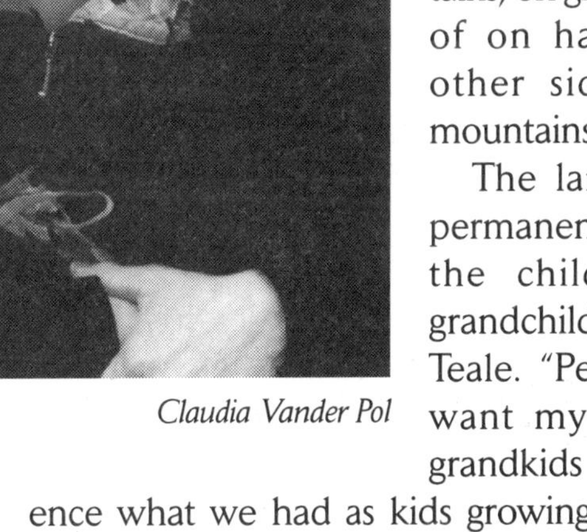

*Claudia Vander Pol*

At one time Claudia even had to weather the storm of people who mistakenly believed that she was growing veal. "We had people coming here and trying to let the cows out. I had one woman stomp into the barn with a cigarette in her mouth demanding to see the baby cows."

But Claudia persisted in studying nutrition and talking to vets to learn how to raise her dairy heifers into high milk-producing cows that she could sell. She is convinced that the best thing her land grows is grass.

"I have had the soil tested a lot," she explains. "I like to know what I've got before I put money into it. The salinity levels [before her fields were diked they were part of the saltwater estuary] are higher in different spots where it has backwashed." She has experimented with leaving certain areas lie fallow and rototilling and replanting others.

Several years ago she hired Chad Felgar to manage the operation. Chad currently raises other people's dairy heifers on consignment until they want them back. Some people want their calves raised on this side of the mountains, on grass, instead of on hay on the other side of the mountains.

The land is in a permanent trust for the children and grandchildren of Ed Teale. "Personally, I want my kids and grandkids to experience what we had as kids growing up here—connection to the land, to how food is raised, to a slower pace of life," says Claudia.

### Preserving Green Space

Several small farmers keep agriculture alive

in the Maxwelton watershed today. Roy Hagglund continues to raise cows as he has done for years. Carolyn Geise raises alpacas. There is a native plant nursery on French Road, a tree farm and nursery on Sills Road and a small Christmas tree-cutting operation on Quade Road. And many people plant large gardens or grow field crops so that valley green space is preserved.

In the upper watershed, the retreat center known as the Marsh House also preserves green space. Owned and operated by Joy Moulton, the seven-acre tract is beautifully arranged with a mix of cultivated gardens, an alder marsh swamp and a naturalized field. People come from all over the United States and Canada to study subjects ranging from music and dance to philosophy and spirituality there.

## A New Organization

In summer 1985, resident and engineer Allen Fitz mapped the watershed. In 1986 he and fellow landowner and writer Todd Peterson did a stream survey of spawning areas and met with biologist Mike Nelson about the disappearance of salmon from Maxwelton Creek.

The following year they were joined by former Mariner baseball star Bruce Bochte, who had moved to the island, and fisheries biologist Russ Orrell. They used the technique of electroshocking the stream to confirm the distribution of fish and identify barriers to fish passage.

The survey information confirmed the need for modification of the tidegates. Working with Diking District #2, and with assistance from Congressman Jack Metcalf and the Department of Fish and Wildlife, funding was secured to replace the faulty tidegates where Maxwelton Creek empties into Puget Sound.

Bruce Bochte's daughter was in Rene Neff's fifth-grade class at the South Whidbey Intermediate School. In 1990 Bruce got Rene and her students interested in planting young salmon in the stream.

A group of parents and educators—Laurie McCollum, Laurie Stanton, Laurie O'Halloran, Rene, Susie Nelson and others—began organizing around the notion of building an outdoor learning center to teach children about salmon and other features of the watershed.

In 1992, Dave Anderson, a local fisherman and soon-to-be state representative from the area, set up and monitored egg boxes in the creek, releasing 60,000 fry into the stream. The following year, fifth-grade students began collecting pennies to buy and preserve land for an outdoor classroom site. Students and members of the newly-formed non-profit organization, the Maxwelton Salmon Adventure, raised over $8,000.

Maxwelton Salmon Adventure

The project gained momentum, and the following year the Salmon Adventure secured $57,000 for the purchase of property on the stream through the Island County Conservation Futures Fund. They purchased 6.3 acres of the Patton land just off French Road behind the Little Brown Church.

## Building the Classroom

The tradition of community barn-raising is well established in Maxwelton. For example, in 1952 the Kinskie home burned to the ground. A year later the community helped Tern Kinskie and his family raise a new house on the old site with lumber cut from their own property and milled in the Evergreen Mill.

In 1996, with the help of a $10,000 donation from the South Whidbey Rotary Club and the direction of Ed Gemkow of Island Construction, the Outdoor Classroom was built with volunteer labor and community support.

"There isn't a lumber or hardware store on Whidbey Island that didn't donate something to the completion of this classroom," says Nancy Scoles, the first teacher at the classroom. "There also isn't a single contractor that didn't donate some of his time. It was really very exciting."

Interpretive trails, a bridge and stream-viewing platforms were added to the classroom site. The covered space outdoors and 30x40 foot enclosed classroom building provide a warm place for activities on those days when cold rain would otherwise make miserable a half-day school outing. The classroom gives children hands-on experience with outdoor life.

"Mrs. Scoles, there is no way I am going to touch a spider!" said the fourth grader.

"That's fine," reassured Nancy Scoles. "But maybe you'd consider looking at it under the microscope."

Later, from the other end of the outdoor classroom came more squeals. "Mrs. Scoles, come here and look. This is so cool! The spider has hairy legs and six eyes!" Mrs. Scoles made her way over to the microscope and realized sometime later that the young girl who had been afraid to touch a spider was ooohing and aaahing at the magnified version of her fear.

The Outdoor Classroom supports about 2,000 student visits a year. A number of those are repeat visits from South Whidbey School District's elementary students. In addition to teaching youngsters, the classroom has served as a community gathering place for schoolteacher retreats and adult community classes.

The Maxwelton Salmon Adventure has broadened its mission to include preservation and protection of salmon and habitat in the watershed. The organization works cooperatively with landowners to identify restoration opportunities, and obtains funding for projects such as the research, writing and publishing of this book.

## The Cycle of Ownership

One of the biggest changes to any rural area is the loss of its old-timers and the homes and other landmarks they have created. Maxwelton has been extremely fortunate in this respect. Many of the original families were large and so at least some members of those families have remained in the area to carry on their stories.

And in the case of a number of families, the second, third or even fourth generation still lives on the original property. That is true for the Kinskie, Green, Wildes, Long, Brixner, Silliman, McDonald, Hagglund and Quade families.

Some watershed land has been purchased by new owners who have a sensitivity to the history of their property. One old-time family and some of these new owners were willing to share their stories.

### The Old Green Place
***John and Becky Williamson***

It would be hard to find someone more enthusiastic about history than John Williamson. He and his wife Becky, Everett Green's youngest daughter, live in Everett's old place on the Maxwelton bluff. John has carefully sorted through all the farming implements in Everett's crowded old barn. John has also done a lot of searching through old photos and letters.

*John Williamson*

"My own family history has not been preserved," explains John. "Becky's family had writers and we have this piece of property. I think it's really important to understand where we've come from."

Next to the house that Becky and John live in is a ramshackle wooden cabin where Becky was raised. It was chock full of everything from old tables to linens. Though many of the things that Everett collected over the years from folks in the area are now in disrepair, John is carefully sorting through everything. Some things go to the dump, some things go into the "save" pile. The perfect caretaker of Everett's treasures has come along and married into the family line.

## The Old Burley Property
### *Carolyn Geise and Bill Jobe*

Bill Jobe was raised on the beach and sought a place with the perfect combination of sky and water. After looking for property "close to Seattle" for two years he and his wife, architect Carolyn Geise, found Leon and Marie Burley's farm on the bluff for sale. "We were excited to find a place that was historic and had so many natural features—a salmon stream, pastures, and mountain and water views," says Carolyn.

Carolyn and Bill are working to return the land to its full agricultural expression. "We can tell this was a much-loved place," says Carolyn. "We are bringing the gardens and fields back to life and are carefully restoring the old house." Experienced farmer Bill Fraser is working with Carolyn and her husband to care for the land and their herd of alpacas.

*Alpacas now share the old Burley farm.*

Carolyn still works full-time in Seattle, so she and Bill often rent their place out to Seattle friends who "could really use some time on a farm." People come for a few days or a week. "One of our guests wrote in the guest book, 'Life flows into us here.' That kind of sums it up for me. I feel really close to my Maker out here. And I feel a responsibility owning the property of the Burleys who I have heard referred to as people who were a kind of 'moral compass' for their community."

## The Old Montgomery Place
### *Virginia Price*

When Virginia Price purchased the Montgomery place on Maxwelton Beach, she never imagined she would become president of the South Whidbey Historical Society and interested in the history of the area.

"When I moved to the island in 1965 to help my mom after dad's death, I needed a place for my kids and me to live. I just kind of fell in love with the old place and was lucky that Jim was still alive to pass on some information about things."

The house was perfect for a young family. It was located on the beach, next to the Maxwelton store, and had lots of bedrooms. "Jim was very pleased to have a family with young children in it breathing life back into the property," says Virginia.

It didn't take Virginia long to become woven into the Maxwelton community. "I needed a babysitter and someone recommended Phyllis Green, oldest daughter of Everett Green. While she was here, she called her dad and told him the toilet was running. Well, Everett was over the next day fixing the toilet and, in the way that only he could do, was sharing stories about the valley. He became my handyman for everything after that."

The first tax record for the house is in 1914. It was built by James Edgar Montgomery, owner of the 1907 store at the end of the Maxwelton dock and the first postmaster of Maxwelton.

James Edgar's great-grandson Dave lives with his wife Eileen on former Mackie family property in the lower Maxwelton watershed.

### Mrs. Hanson's Place
***Gregg and Linda Ridder***

"We were looking for a sense of community, but not the gated kind," says Gregg Ridder, retired chemist for Proctor and Gamble. "We were ready to get out of the Ohio heat and humidity. We love the weather, the big trees, and the diversity of people and economic situations. It's a *real* place."

Gregg and Linda bought the old Hanson property on Sills Road in 2001 and are looking forward to becoming part of the Maxwelton community as soon as their home is built. Mrs. Hanson's two sons built the original house in 1913. As was typical of Maxwelton properties, there was also a shed and a chicken house.

Mrs. Hanson lived on the property until 1947. With the help of Todd Soli, the Ridders arranged for Goosefoot Community Fund to move the old house to the property of former renters Tim and Leslie Jackson. The Ridders now have a cleared property to build on, and the Jacksons have an historic building to tend.

### The Old Parsons Place
***Patty and Loren Imes***

John and Nellie Parsons took over the lands homesteaded in 1880 by Pat Quinn. They established a tradition of careful farming that has been carried on by all succeeding owners. Clyde Driscoll owned the farm after the Parsons.

"I remember Clyde's big horses: Babe, Bell and Bubbles," said Shirley Hjort Gillette. "He would come and mow our hay with the horses. I can still hear the harnesses jingling and the clackity-clack of the horses. They were so gentle you could walk right underneath them. I also remember sitting on top of them. They were so big my legs were sticking straight out."

*The old Hanson house was moved to a new location in 2002. Goosefoot Community Fund's Affordable Housing program facilitated the move.*

Bill and Helen Bone bought the place from Clyde in 1958 and raised cattle. "I wanted a little farm and to enjoy the land, as my father and grandfather had," says Bill. In 1999 the Bones sold the land to Patty and Loren Imes, knowing that they intended to keep the place as a working farm.

Patty Imes grew up on a dairy farm in Wisconsin. She and Loren are working to establish an organic farm with U-pick berries, beef cows, chickens, and nut and fruit trees. "We feel lucky to have worked with Bill. He taught us how to work with cattle and has been a wealth of information on everything," says Patty.

**The Old Patton Place**
***Arthur and Emma Applegate***

John Sr. and John Patton, Jr. were long-time farmers and community members in the Maxwelton watershed. Their poultry farm on the northwest bluff above the former saltwater estuary employed many Maxwelton people over the years. John Sr. passed away in 1954 and John Jr. and his wife Dorothy operated the farm until their retirement in 1989. John Jr. cared for the land as carefully in its transition from farm to real estate as he did during the heyday of its life as a poultry farm.

Slowly, portions of the original farm, especially those down on the flats, were sold to help pay the growing real estate taxes. In the years since John Jr.'s death in 1994, other parcels of the bluff-top property have sold.

*Three generations of homes on the original Quinn homestead. Counterclockwise from above: Parsons, Bone, Imes.*

Arthur and Emma Applegate are building a home for themselves and their two school-aged children on the seven-acre site where the senior Patton home originally stood. Arthur has been working out of a home office for over a decade, so he is not concerned about the commute.

"We were looking for view property with enough sun for a garden, yet with forest around," says Arthur. "We appreciate the fact that this is an historic site for the valley."

*Fifth-graders explore the culvert that empties Maxwelton Creek into the Sound. Below, an aerial view of the outfall of the creek.*

A Journey Through the Maxwelton Watershed

Chapter 11

# Looking to the Future

As the largest watershed in Island County, Maxwelton is a microcosm of rural watersheds throughout the Pacific Northwest. It contains no cities or towns, but its year-round creek was historically important to both native peoples and early settlers. And today it plays a crucial role in preserving rural amenities like clean water, open space, wildlife and farmland.

Longtime farmers, a few loggers and an increasing number of city folk seeking a country life find themselves sharing resources and fence lines. Somehow all of these political and personality types must find ways to work together to shape the future of their small area.

Several key issues are symbolic of the challenges Maxwelton residents face to protect and preserve the quality of life in their watershed.

## The Persistent Beavers

Most farmers in the Maxwelton watershed encounter beaver on a regular basis. In the lower watershed there is a huge colony of beaver with multiple dams and lodges in the southeast corner of the modern-day marsh. "I walk our field every day to monitor beaver activity," says Bill Fraser, who is working with Carolyn Geise and Bill Jobe. Bill Steiner concurs with Fraser that daily maintenance is the only way to stay ahead of them, but adds that often that isn't enough.

"You want a demoralizing experience," says Cary Peterson, president of the Whidbey Camano Land Trust, "try and keep up with beavers for a week. You can't do it."

The Land Trust, dedicated to preserving special lands in Island County, received a donation in 1999 of 24 acres south and east of Miller Lake. As Cary says, "We really understand the challenges of farmers and other landowners in the valley because we are now landowners ourselves."

On an August day, Cary is making the rounds among the four beaver dams on their property. Her goal is to keep enough water flowing through the dams so that neighboring properties upstream are not flooded. "You can't work on your land in a vacuum," she says. "What you do affects everyone around you." The Land Trust has obtained a permit from the state Department of Fish and Wildlife to modify beaver

*A beaver dam near Miller Lake.*

dams on their property.

As she is working, she pulls out big handfuls of small, intertwined twigs and throws them atop a five-foot-high pile of twigs from previous days of dam destroying. It takes a while before the water begins to flow through the structure. When she gets down to the level of mud and peat, she explains, "The beavers scoop out huge clods of mud, grass and peat from side channels, float them over to the dam where they've already placed sticks and twigs, and pack them against the sticks. They are tireless. They don't have anything to do except build dams every night."

Cary and volunteer Chuck Bower are working on a system that might lessen the need for beaver vigilance. Using techniques that have been tried in other places, they are installing flow pipes into dams. First, they open up the dam. Then they install a ten-foot section of four- to five-inch diameter drain pipe with a metal cage over the intake opening to prevent the beavers from plugging it up. Finally, they hold it in place with six-foot-long rebar.

When the beavers rebuild the dam, they build right over the top of the pipe. Their dam blocks some flow, but water keeps moving through the drainage pipe. Cary and Chuck's goal is to perfect the system and begin to share it with other landowners in the watershed.

"We're trying to be a model for how land can be restored and maintained," explains Cary. "We removed the blackberries that were choking a tributary of the stream. Now, with the help of

*Beavers use peat and twigs to build dams near Miller Lake.*

AmeriCorps volunteers, we're planting native vegetation like willow, alder, hawthorn, Indian plum, bitter cherry and Pacific crab apple."

While a challenge to landowners, beavers actually create good salmon habitat. As fisheries biologist Jim Lichatowich writes in *Salmon Without Rivers,* beavers and salmon "co-evolved in Northwest watersheds over thousands of years."[26]

And contrary to popular belief, beaver dams are not a fish barrier. Lichatowich describes how beavers' activities create pools and wetlands which store sediments, organic material and nutrients for slow release into a system. The mere presence of their dams, especially in the upper watershed, reduces the fluctuation of water in a small creek like Maxwelton. There is a "reservoir" for constant flow even in the dry months of summer.

## Were They Always Here?

There appears to be some controversy about whether beavers existed in the early settlement days of Maxwelton. Joe Long, who arrived in the watershed with his mother and brothers in 1926, wrote a few comments about Maxwelton Creek in 1999. "To the best of my knowledge there were no beavers in the creek. There was no building material for their dams. Every few years the creek would be cleaned of mud and sediment. Herb Gildow brought in his dragline and cleaned the whole creek." Lincoln Wildes also did not remember seeing beavers as a boy growing up in the valley.

Joe is a farmer and observant about the land he tends. Lincoln is a hunter and a logger and has spent his entire life outdoors. Their comments are puzzling, but noteworthy. Hudson's Bay Company trapping in the early 1800s in general did not decimate beaver populations on Whidbey Island. In fact, Richard White writes that "George Gibbs, a government official and ethnologist, claimed that there were as many beaver in the 1850s as there had ever been."[27]

By all rights, beavers should have been in both the upper and lower valleys of the Maxwelton watershed when Wildes and Long were boys. Long may have the explanation for the phenomenon: "There was no habitat." The creek was regularly being dredged. Regulations today prevent dredging, making the creek more favorable for beaver activity.

If there were not *wild* beaver, there were beaver farms by the 1930s. Lincoln Wildes remembers that they hired kids to cut willow to feed their captive animals. Kris Ravetz, who lives at the lower edge of Campbell Road, has old concrete abutments on her property from an early beaver operation.

Eventually, of course, some of the beavers escaped. Whether they joined wild beavers migrating into the area from other parts of Whidbey Island or whether they alone resettled the Maxwelton watershed, there is definitely a stable beaver population in the valley now.

Most landowners in the watershed have had some experience with beavers. If the story we tell about beavers is that there is no way to control them, they will likely accommodate that prediction. However, if the story is of people working together to solve the problems created by the industrious beaver, an entirely different scenario emerges.

## *Creating Community*

"We used to know everybody down here," explains Gerry Brixner Miller. "Now we hardly know our neighbors."

Many things have changed. But one thing that has survived all of these changes, and that still brings people together, is the Maxwelton Fourth of July parade.

The 2002 Fourth of July parade was the largest and longest in its ninety-year history. According to parade organizer Dana Gilroy, six years ago it was twenty minutes in length and in 2002 it was 50 minutes long. The 2002 Grand Marshall, Myron Brixner, was astounded by the size of the parade. "Why when we were kids, it was hardly anything," he says.

As far as Dana is aware, the parade has been held every year since 1912, except for a few years during World War I and World War II. "No one knows for sure exactly how the first parade started, but most people believe that P. H. Mackie started it back in 1912. Now it's a tradition. Many of us who have been doing this year after year are convinced that people would still come and line up even if we didn't organize it."

*Grand Marshall, Myron Brixner*

With attendance running about six to seven thousand people in a tiny two-block, dead-end area, organization is undoubtedly a good thing.

Fire trucks, children on tricycles and bicycles, old cars, politicians, clowns, dance troupes, musicians and family floats have been a tradition for years. For the past several years the "Procession of the Species" part of the parade has featured homemade costumes of different native plant and animal species in the Maxwelton watershed. In 2002 many of the animal and plant puppets were hoisted onto twenty-foot poles and "danced" down the parade route.

There are other community-building events in the valley as well. In response to a Washington Conservation Commission report citing the tidegates as a barrier to fish passage, the Maxwelton Salmon Adventure received funding in 2001 to hire professional biologists and hydrologists to study the lower watershed.

An important feature of the Maxwelton Lower Reach & Fish Passage Feasibility Study was landowner involvement. "We didn't want to conduct the study in a vacuum," says project director Laura Fox. "We've worked hard to involve landowners and genuinely want to find solutions that are about the preservation of both human and wildlife interests."

The collection of oral histories from watershed residents and the writing and publishing of this book were funded by a contract with the Puget Sound Water Quality Action Team. Community-building has been at the very heart of this project.

There are other examples, too. The Maxwelton Creek Co-housing project and the Drummuir development model new ways of using land for closer-knit communities and preserving open space. In 2002, a Labor Day "Sills Road barbecue" was held to help neighbors in that area get to know one another. And every summer, countless family reunions are held that honor the ongoing presence of valley families.

So it is true that population growth and greater societal mobility has made it harder to get to know one's neighbors in Maxwelton. But the story that might be told about how that challenge is being met is that a number of efforts are underway to keep community spirit strong.

*Procession of the Species, 2002.*

## The Return of Salmon

Since the 1980s, a number of studies have indicated that large, historic salmon runs no longer exist in the stream. There are strong feelings, both positive and negative, about whether an effort should be made to re-establish them.

"I can't think of anything that gets kids more excited than working with salmon fry and hoping an adult salmon will return to Maxwelton Creek," says fifth-grade teacher Rene Neff, longtime Salmon Adventure president.

Some landowners in the valley are also excited about the possibility that spawning salmon might again cross their land. "One of the reasons we bought land here was that our property had a salmon creek on it," explains Nancy Scoles, who with her husband Steve bought the old Nourse place. "Salmon are symbolic of a healthy Pacific Northwest ecosystem."

For every landowner enthusiastic about living near a salmon stream, there are others fearful of what governmental regulations might do to their ability to farm if substantial numbers of salmon return.

"Environmental restrictions are driving small farmers out," says Claudia Vander Pol. "We're afraid the salmon issue will make things worse."

"Outsiders live on their lots and we own their greenbelt," says Bill Steiner. "We love our land and we need to be able to farm it."

The recent Feasibility Study concluded that a number of factors affect fish passage and production in addition to the tidegates.

The former estuary no longer has an adequate salt- and fresh-water mixing zone which juvenile salmon need to transition to the salt water of Puget Sound. The temperature of fresh water in the lower creek is often too high for juvenile fish and lacks sufficient levels of dissolved oxygen.

The study proposes a number of alternatives to help salmon return to the watershed, such as replacing the current tidegate, installing a box culvert under Maxwelton Road, building or removing various dikes and acquiring conservation easements or land of willing landowners.

"Any actual changes will depend on the participation of landowners," explains Laura Fox. "We will seek funding for the restoration alternative selected by the community."

The passion of Salmon Adventure co-president John Hastings is plants. "Native plants in the watershed are crucial in dealing with water issues," says John. "The quality and quantity of water is directly related to the plant communities found here." John is creating a comprehensive database of watershed plants and hopes to work with landowners interested in restoring their native plant communities.

A hundred-year visioning process is another part of the history project. Watershed residents will have a chance to say what they'd like to see fade away, what should stay the same, and what positive changes they'd like to see in the future. Residents will determine how the Maxwelton watershed proceeds from this point forward.

The story being perpetuated here is not that salmon should replace farmlands, but rather that people are looking for long-term solutions and inviting everyone to determine what role, if any, salmon should play in the next century of the watershed.

## A Love for the Land

The love for the valley and its beauty has kept generations of families living in Maxwelton. The number of fourth- and fifth-generation families in this small area is extraordinary in this day and age of mobility. Whether talking to an eighty-year-old resident or a recent arrival, people speak similar refrains about Maxwelton.

"I just love the marsh," says Leon Burley in a 1988 family videotape.

"This is a magical place," says Carolyn Geise, new owner of the Leon and Marie Burley place.

"I love the combination of tall trees, view, and

garden space," responds Arthur Applegate, new owner of the old Patton place.

"I left once for two weeks for a job in Seattle. There's no place like this on earth," says Darrell Green.

"The wide-openness of the valley, the spacious agricultural corridor, the phenomenal water-holding capacity, the fact that it's a salmon stream . . . Maxwelton is just a special place," says Cary Peterson with the Whidbey Camano Land Trust.

"The light in the valley—whether looking at the sun setting over the Olympics or dawn in the marsh—is magical," says Rene Neff of the Maxwelton Salmon Adventure.

Though there are complex decisions to be made about land use priorities, it is clear that the preservation of the valley's beauty and health is a unifying theme. To a person, landowners would rejoice in a hundred-year vision that results in a landscape similar to what is visible today. And to a person, they would agree that the watershed should remain healthy enough to support wildlife and clean water.

A walk out into the marsh of the upper watershed about dusk on an August evening remains a nearly timeless experience. The temperature drops nearly ten degrees during the descent from Maxwelton Road onto the marsh flats. The evening dew on high grass brushes off onto pant legs and shoes.

About a quarter of a mile from the road, nearly to the shores of Miller Lake, one becomes aware of a thousand sounds beyond the swishing of moving grass. An old bullfrog croaks from the shore of Miller Lake. A great blue heron coming in to roost pierces the night with an ancient squawk. Dogs bark at a distant farm. The high-pitched whistles of duck wings play a violin symphony overhead.

As dusk makes the slow turn to darkness, one's eyes focus on shapes instead of colors. The silhouettes of dead cottonwoods along the shore of the flooded lake stand sharp against the western horizon—sentinels silenced by the persistent beavers. Looking west, one sees surprisingly few farm lights—just the looming blackness of one of Whidbey Island's highest hills. A streak of light across the northern sky is a Perseid meteor making its mid-August pilgrimage into oblivion.

It is possible to hear cars moving along State Route 525, a little over a mile away, but mostly the observer feels immersed in a time and place that is far from the bustle of the twenty-first century. This is the best of rural America.

The watershed has survived, in relative health, the immense changes of moving from an age of horses and hand labor to the age of machines and telecommuting. Standing by the marsh at the end of a summer day, it's hard to guess at the changes another century will bring.

One can only hope that the combined visions of old-timers and newcomers will give children of the twenty-second century a Maxwelton watershed that is as much a source of sustenance and pride as the valley is to landowners and residents today.

# Where Many Rivers Meet

by David Whyte

All the water below me came from above.
All the clouds living in the mountains
gave it to the rivers,
who gave it to the sea, which was their dying.

And so I float on cloud become water,
central sea surrounded by white mnountains,
the water salt, once fresh,
cloud fall and stream rush, tree roots and tide bank
leading to the rivers mouths
and the mouths of the rivers sing into the sea,
the stories buried in the mountains
give out into the sea
and the sea remembers
and sings back
from the depths
where nothing is forgotten.

*Where Many Rivers Meet,* Many Rivers Press, 1990

---

# Chain of Life

A song by Susan Osborn

I see where I am now
At the table of the harvest;
Before me went the plow
And the trees that grew to forest.
There's a chain of life behind me
From here to the horizon;
Each generation rising
From the one that went before.

I hear the young ones coming
Hearts open and hopeful;
Their dreams will be unfolding
On the ground we leave behind us.
Take the best of what you're given
Make a joyous dance to living;
And somewhere in the spinning
You too will sing this song.

I'm makin' my shoulders strong
for the young to stand upon;
Steppin' lightly on the backs of those
Who hold me up.
It's a chain of life unending
Ever new and ever bending;
Grateful is the heart for the chance
to be alive. . .

# Footnotes

1. Russell Link, WA Department of Fish & Wildlife, unpublished material, 2002
2. Bruce Brown, *Mountain in the Clouds,* 1982, A Touchstone Book, Simon & Schuster, Inc., NY
3. Herbert C. Fish and William Shelton, "Our Totem Maker," unpublished manuscript from the 1920's
4. Dorothy Neil, *By Canoe and Sailing Ship They Came,* 1989, Spindrift Publishing Co., Oak Harbor, WA
5. *Sails, Steamships and Sea Captains–Settlement, Trade and Transportation in Island County Between 1850 and 1900,* Island County Historical Society, 1993, Coupeville, WA
6. Edmond S. Meany, "Chief Patkainum", Washington Historical Quarterly, January 1924, Vol. XV, #1
7. Lorna Cherry, *South Whidbey and Its People, Volume I,* 1983, South Whidbey Historical Society, Langley, WA, page 74
8. *A Centennial Look at the Boy who Became the Father of Langley, Jacob Anthes 1868-1939,* 1999, South Whidbey Historical Society, Langley, WA.
9. Todd Peterson, "Hair-raising times recalled by logger," April 27, 1982, South Whidbey Record
10. From personal correspondence of Clair Mackie, grandson of T. S. Mackie
11. From research and report done by Donna Humphreys in 1998-99 for The Whidbey Institute, Clinton, WA
12. Richard White, *Land Use, Environment, and Social Change: The Shaping of Island County, Washington,* 1992, University of Washington Press, Seattle, WA, Page 116
13. Ibid., page 118
14. Northwest Hydraulic Consultants, "Maxwelton Lower Reach and Fish Passage Feasibility Study," September 2002 draft
15. Ibid.
16. Nancy Donnelly, "The Formative Years," 1976, Washington State Arts Committee and the Sno-Isle Regional Library, page 46
17. Todd Peterson, "Great Depression wasn't quite so depressing," July 27, 1982, South Whidbey Record
18. Bruce Brown, op. cit.
19. Jim Lichatowich, *Salmon Without Rivers: A History of the Pacific Salmon Crisis,* 1999, Island Press, Washington, D.C., page 12
20. Brown, op. cit.
21. Nancy Donnelly, op. cit.
22. Much of the factual information about wildlife in this chapter was taken from information written by Russell Link, WA Department of Fish and Wildlife, 2002
23. Richard White, op. cit.
24. Ibid.
25. Figure from research librarian, Sno-Isle Regional Library System, branch in Freeland, WA ; outlying areas include those beyond King County.
26. Jim Lichatowich, op. cit.
27. Richard White, op. cit.

Acknowledgement for background interviews with reference librarians in the Northwest Collections room of the Everett Public Library, 2002

# Bibliography

Brian Astwood, *Chief William Shelton's Legends of the Everett Totem Pole,* 1996, first published by the Tulalip Tribes, 1923 and 1935, Everett, WA

Bruce Brown, *Mountain in the Clouds,* 1982, A Touchstone Book, Simon and Schuster, Inc., NY

Pat Buckley and Barry Bjork, "The Nisqually Delta: Its Place in History," July 31, 2002 lecture at Nisqually National Wildlife Refuge, WA

The Chautauqua Institution web site: http://www.chautauqua-inst.org/about.html

Lorna Cherry, *South Whidbey and Its People, Volume I,* 1983, South Whidbey Historical Society, Langley, WA

Lorna Cherry, *South Whidbey and Its People, Volume II,* 1985, South Whidbey Historical Society, Langley, WA

Nancy Donnelly, "The Formative Years," 1976, Washington State Arts Committee and the Sno-Isle Regional Library

Hakluyt Society of London, *The Voyage of George Vancouver, 1791-1795,* four volumes edited by W. Kaye Lamb, 1984

Herbert C. Fish and William Shelton ,"Our Totem Maker," unpublished manuscript from the 1920's

E. M. Hawes and Lou Clark, *Island County, a World Beater,* originally published in 1911, added to and copyrighted by Elizabeth R. Dodge, 1968, reprinted in 1974 and 1979, Clinton, WA

Donna Humphreys, Chautauqua research and report done in 1999 for The Whidbey Institute, Clinton, WA

Island County Historical Society, *Sails, Steamships and Sea Captains–Settlement, Trade and Transportation in Island County Between 1850 and 1900,* 1993, Coupeville, WA

George A. Kellogg, *A History of Whidbey's Island,* 1934 reprinted 2001, Island County Historical Society, Coupeville, WA

Jim Lichatowich, *Salmon Without Rivers: A History of the Pacific Salmon Crisis,* 1999, Island Press, Washington, D.C.

Edmond S. Meany, "Chief Patkainum," Washington Historical Quarterly, January 1924, Vol. XV, #1

Dorothy Neil, *By Canoe and Sailing Ship They Came,* 1989, Spindrift Publishing Co., Oak Harbor, WA

Northwest Hydraulic Consultants, "Maxwelton Lower Reach and Fish Passage Feasibility Study," September 2002 draft

South Whidbey Historical Society, "A centennial look at the boy who became the father of Langley," 1999, Langley, WA

Gordon Speck, *Northwest Explorations,* 1954 & 1970, Binfords & Mort, Portland, OR

University of Washington PRISM web site: http://www.prism.washington.edu/vps/intrface/multigal/graphics_animations/animations/ps_glaciation2.html

James R. Warren, *Where Mountains Meet the Sea–an Illustrated History of Puget Sound,* 1986, Windsor Publications, Inc., Seattle, WA

Washington State Department of Ecology, Puget Sound Shorelines web site: http://www.ecy.wa.gov/programs/sea/pugetsound/tour/history.html

Robert C. Wing and Gordon Newell, *Peter Puget,* 1979, Gray Beard Publishing, Seattle, WA

Richard White, *Land Use, Environment, and Social Change: The Shaping of Island County Washington,* 1992, University of Washington Press, Seattle, WA

---

# The Production Team

**Ann Linnea** did the majority of the research and oral interviews for this book and wrote the book under a contract with the Maxwelton Salmon Adventure. She is a biologist by training, with certificates in elementary and secondary education. She has worked as a newspaper journalist, a naturalist for the U.S. Forest Service and wrote a hiking and cross-country skiing guide to the northern Utah mountains. Her previous books are *Deep Water Passage, A Spiritual Journey at Mid-Life and Teaching Kids to Love the Earth.* Her work appears in several anthologies.

Ann is co-owner of PeerSpirit, Inc., an educational firm presenting seminars for individuals, groups and businesses which teach communication skills. Ann leads wilderness seminars and trips for PeerSpirit that combine adventure with personal development. She has delivered keynote speeches and workshops at many national conferences and co-authored a series of booklets for PeerSpirit.

Contact Ann at (360) 331-3580 or through www.peerspirit.com.

**Vicki Grayson Liden** of Grayson Design did the layout and design of the book and cover, including preparation of all images and graphics. Vicki specializes in fine art reproduction, product photography, web and graphic design, catalog production, online stores, and digital photo retouch. She works from her "electronic cottage" on Whidbey island. Contact Vicki at: (360) 321-5929 or by e-mail at grayson@whidbey.com. www.graysondesign.net

**Susan Zwinger** provided illustrations for the cover, the Jacob Anthes cabin, and the Vashon Glacier. She is a critically-acclaimed natural history writer, an environmental activist, teacher, artist and illustrator. Her book *Stalking the Ice Dragon* won the Governor's Author Award in 1992. She lives on Whidbey Island and travels extensively.

**Nancy Waddell**, editor and project coordinator, has worked as a public involvement specialist in local government in Snohomish County, Washington, and Portland, Oregon. She graduated from Connecticut College with a major in Zoology but spent most of her college years in the campus theater and worked off-Broadway in New York City for many years. She is now a project manager for non-profit organizations and lives in the Maxwelton watershed of Whidbey Island.

*Members of the Advisory Committee meeting at the former Burley place.*

This book was written using Microsoft Word 98 for Mac and designed in Adobe PageMaker 6.5 and Adobe Photoshop. The main text font is Jaeger Daily News ITP, with chapter titles in Sanvito and headings in Serif Gothic.

The book was printed by Snohomish Publishing, Snohomish, Washington.
Thanks to Ralph Heiner for his advice and gracious assistance.

# Index

# Index

# Index

# Photo Credits

Photos by Ann Linnea and Nancy Waddell or from the Internet unless noted below. Scanning, retouching and adaptations by Grayson Design.

Robert Barnes 55 lower, 86 top
Bill Bone collection 85 right
Myron Brixner collection 1, 23, 27 lower, 28 lower, 38 top, 39, 40, 41, 53 top, 62, 67,70 top
Kris Collins 51 left
Doreen Delano collection 51 right and bottom, 52, 68
Carolyn Geise 83
Imes family 85 top
Island County Public Works (Matt Nash) 4, 47
Carla Jolley 58
Lea Kouba 56
Mary Sue Lile collection 50 top
Leland Long collection 61 lower
McDonald-Tinker collection 46 lower
in *Northwest Explorations* 16, 18 lower, 19, 20
Northwest Hydraulic Consultants 36, 93
Wilma O'Nan 59, 69
Todd Peterson (in *South Whidbey Record*) 34, 53 lower, 61 top
Ed Severinghaus 57
Silliman Family collection 3, 7, 17, 28 top, 45, 46 top, 55 top, 74, 95, 101
South Whidbey Historical Society 25, 31, 38 lower, 48, 75
Joyce Terrell 6
Sally Thompson 80, 81
Williamson-Green collection 14, 21, 27 top, 32, 54, 82
Our apologies for any mis-identification.

*And the journey continues…*